Grand Finales

A MODERNIST VIEW OF PLATED DESSERTS

Grand Finales

TISH BOYLE and TIMOTHY MORIARTY
Editors of Chocolatier *and* Pastry Art & Design

Introduction by
MICHAEL SCHNEIDER
Editor-in-Chief, Chocolatier *and* Pastry Art & Design

Photography by
JOHN UHER

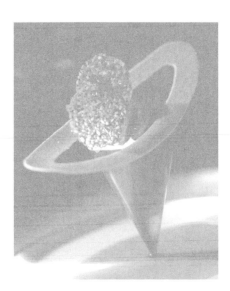

A MODERNIST VIEW OF PLATED DESSERTS

VNR Van Nostrand Reinhold
I T P® A Division of International Thomson Publishing Inc.

New York • Albany • Bonn • Boston • Detroit • London • Madrid • Melbourne
Mexico City • Paris • San Francisco • Singapore • Tokyo • Toronto

Plate credits:
page xvi, Cyclamen Studio
page 21, Rosenthal
page 32, Oggetti
page 40, Jena Glass
page 46, Rosenthal
page 56, Annie Glass
page 66, Annie Glass
page 77, Cyclamen Studio
page 82, Bernardaud
page 91, Studio D'Or
page 100, Mexican Gift House
page 104, Villeroy & Boch
page 115, Villeroy & Boch
page 124, Opus
page 132, Mexican Gift House
page 142, Villeroy & Boch
page 145, Bernardaud
page 149, Villeroy & Boch
page 178, Rosenthal
page 204, Dan Levy
page 218, Annie Glass
page 240, Sasaki.

I(T)P® an International Thomson Publishing Company
The ITP logo is a registered trademark used herein under license

Printed in the United States of America

For more information, contact:

Van Nostrand Reinhold
115 Fifth Avenue
New York, NY 10003

Chapman & Hall GmbH
Pappelallee 3
69469 Weinheim
Germany

Chapman & Hall
2-6 Boundary Row
London
SE1 8HN
United Kingdom

International Thomson Publishing Asia
221 Henderson Road #05-10
Henderson Building
Singapore 0315

Thomas Nelson Australia
102 Dodds Street
South Melbourne, 3205
Victoria, Australia

International Thomson Publishing Japan
Hirakawacho Kyowa Building, 3F
2-2-1 Hirakawacho
Chiyoda-ku, 102 Tokyo
Japan

Nelson Canada
1120 Birchmount Road
Scarborough, Ontario
Canada M1K 5G4

International Thomson Editores
Seneca 53
Col. Polanco
11560 Mexico D.F. Mexico

1 2 3 4 5 6 7 8 9 10   RRD - ROA   01 00 99 98 97

Library of Congress Cataloging-in-Publication Data

A modernist view of plated desserts: grand finales / [compiled by] Tish Boyle and Timothy Moriarty; created by Michael Schneider; photography by John Uher.
     p. cm.
    Includes index.
    ISBN 0-442-02547-5
    1. Desserts. 2. Pastry. I. Boyle, Tish. II. Moriarty, Timothy.

TX773.G682   1997
97–24171
641.8'6—dc21

97-24171
CIP

http://www.vnr.com
product discounts • free email newsletters
software demos • online resources

email: **info@vnr.com**

A service of I(T)P®

ACKNOWLEDGMENTS

First and foremost, my thanks to the richly talented and extremely good-tempered pastry chefs who made this book possible. I count many of them as my good friends. To Carole Harlam and Faith Robyn Fernbach, the troubleshooters who tested many of these difficult recipes with good humor, patience, and precision. To Mark Kammerer and Stephanie Banyas, for their impeccable attention to detail. To Judy Prince and Fran Shinagel of J.B. Prince for the great book party and for their continued support. To John Uher, the Czar of Dessert Photography. To Michael Schneider for having so much faith in me. And finally, to my husband Dick Eggleston, for his encouragement, love, and sense of humor.

TB

My sincere thanks to each of the chefs whose work is represented here; all were supremely generous with their time and expertise. Thanks also to the public relations staffs, management, and chefs of the Four Seasons Hotels in Palm Beach and Beverly Hills, the Las Vegas Hilton, the Ritz-Carlton Chicago, and the Phoenecian in Scottsdale. Special thanks to Melissa Rosati, for listening and advising, and to Faith Robyn Fernbach, who compiled the source table and lent vital assistance in the preparation of the manuscript. Thanks also to Judy Prince and Rennis Garner of J.B. Prince in New York, Karen Deutsh of LaMalle Cookware in New York, Daphna Epstein, Matthew Stevens, Stephanie Banyas, Mary Goodbody, and Janice Wald Henderson. And as always, thanks and love to Ryan, Evan and, especially, Geri.

TM

CONTENTS

RECIPE CONTENTS

"Art doesn't come in measured quantities: it's got to be too much or it's not enough."

PAULINE KAEL

"Is the pursuit of chocolate a right or a privilege? Does the notion of chocolate preclude the concept of free will?"

SANDRA BOYNTON

CHAPTER ONE

PURE MODERNISM

MANGO BERRY FOOL

KRISTA KERN

Pastry Chef, *Three Fish, Westerly, Rhode Island.*

The madness of Modernism comes to life in this colorful, calamitous plate. A mango fool is served with raspberry sorbet in its center and berries affixed to its side, with a brown sugar shortbread as its base and shaped, dried mangoes as witnesses. Raspberry, mango, and blackberry coulis also call the tune. "A fool? Okay. I like doing it with a wink, a little nod," says Krista Kern. "I'm not above that."

YIELD: 8 SERVINGS

Special Equipment:
Eight 3" high (7.6 cm) timbale molds
One silicone baking mat

MANGO FOOL			
	2	2	ripe mangoes, peeled and pitted
	1 liq oz	30 ml	cold water
	3 sheets	7.5 g	gelatin, soaked in water
	1 Tbs	15 ml	lime juice
	1 pt	473 ml	crème fraîche
	1.8 oz	50 g	granulated sugar
	8 liq oz	237 ml	heavy cream

1. In a food processor, purée mangoes and transfer to a large bowl.

2. In a small saucepan, heat water until warm. Drain gelatin, add to water, and stir until dissolved. Stir in lime juice. Whisk gelatin mixture into mango purée. Whisk in crème fraîche and sugar.

3. In a mixer with a whisk attachment, whip heavy cream to soft peaks. Whisk one-half of the whipped cream into the mango mixture; fold in the remaining whipped cream. Cover and refrigerate until ready to assemble the timbales.

RASPBERRY SORBET			
	4 pts	1.9 lt	raspberries
	3 Tbs	45 ml	simple syrup (50%)
	1 Tbs	15 ml	lemon juice
	4 liq oz	118 ml	water

1. In a food processor, purée raspberries. Add the remaining ingredients and process until just combined. Transfer to a bowl, cover, and refrigerate until cold, about 2 hours.

2. Process the mixture in an ice cream machine according to manufacturer's instructions. Transfer the sorbet to a container, cover, and place in freezer.

CONE OF SILENCE

DONALD WRESSELL

Executive Pastry Chef, *Four Seasons Hotel, Beverly Hills, California.*

This presentation has been much admired ever since Donald Wressell entered a version of it in competition years ago. Professionals and home chefs alike wondered, How does he get the cone to stand up like that? The secret lies in a bottom-heavy chocolate cone anchored with a drop of chocolate that is concealed in sauce. The flavor lives up to the spectacle: gianduja Bavarian flavored with Frangelico and praline paste is nestled inside the cone, and accompanied by Manjari ice cream, burnt orange sauce (camouflage), and a honey wafer. "People say to me, does it kill you to see customers break it and eat it? It doesn't, because I had my fun making it," says Wressell. "That is where my interest in the plate lies. I then pass it off to the diner and hope that he or she will take a moment to admire it."

YIELD: 14 SERVINGS

Special Equipment:
Fourteen plastic cone molds, 3.5 oz (103 ml) capacity with a 2.5" (6.3 cm) diameter opening
Silicone baking mat

CHOCOLATE CONES	24 oz	680 g	*bittersweet chocolate, melted and tempered*

1. Ladle chocolate into one of the cones to fill completely. Turn the cone upside down on a rack and allow excess to drip out. Let the cone set at room temperature for one hour. Refrigerate for at least 15 minutes.

2. Remove the cone from the refrigerator and dislodge it from the mold. Anchor the cone to the center of a dessert plate with a small amount of chocolate (see photos below). Lean the cone against 2 pieces of Plexiglas glued together at right angles until set. Repeat with the remaining cones.

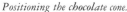
Positioning the chocolate cone.

CONE OF SILENCE

DONALD WRESSELL

Executive Pastry Chef, *Four Seasons Hotel, Beverly Hills, California.*

This presentation has been much admired ever since Donald Wressell entered a version of it in competition years ago. Professionals and home chefs alike wondered, How does he get the cone to stand up like that? The secret lies in a bottom-heavy chocolate cone anchored with a drop of chocolate that is concealed in sauce. The flavor lives up to the spectacle: gianduja Bavarian flavored with Frangelico and praline paste is nestled inside the cone, and accompanied by Manjari ice cream, burnt orange sauce (camouflage), and a honey wafer. "People say to me, does it kill you to see customers break it and eat it? It doesn't, because I had my fun making it," says Wressell. "That is where my interest in the plate lies. I then pass it off to the diner and hope that he or she will take a moment to admire it."

YIELD: 14 SERVINGS

Special Equipment:
Fourteen plastic cone molds, 3.5 oz (103 ml) capacity with a 2.5" (6.3 cm) diameter opening
Silicone baking mat

CHOCOLATE CONES	24 oz	680 g	*bittersweet chocolate, melted and tempered*

1. Ladle chocolate into one of the cones to fill completely. Turn the cone upside down on a rack and allow excess to drip out. Let the cone set at room temperature for one hour. Refrigerate for at least 15 minutes.

2. Remove the cone from the refrigerator and dislodge it from the mold. Anchor the cone to the center of a dessert plate with a small amount of chocolate (see photos below). Lean the cone against 2 pieces of Plexiglas glued together at right angles until set. Repeat with the remaining cones.

Positioning the chocolate cone.

1. Combine the sugar, water, and vanilla bean pods and seeds; let rest overnight.

2. Strain the vanilla pods out of the sugar mixture. Place the sugar mixture in a saucepan with the egg yolks and whites; cook gently, stirring, until the mixture reaches 185°F (85°C). Transfer to a mixer and whip until cool.

3. Fold in the whipped cream.

SPRAYING CHOCOLATE

17.6 oz	*500 g*	*cocoa butter*
17.6 oz	*500 g*	*Valrhona Manjari couverture*
17.6 oz	*500 g*	*Valrhona cocoa paste*

1. Melt the cocoa butter, couverture, and cocoa paste separately.

2. Combine and keep in a warm, dry area until needed for spraying.

ASSEMBLY

White chocolate gears sprayed with green cocoa butter
Pulled sugar rods

1. Line the demi-sphere molds with the chocolate ice cream, packing it in well to ensure that there are no air bubbles. Cover the ice cream with a thin coat of raspberry coulis. Freeze until set.

2. Pipe in the vanilla parfait almost to the top of the mold. Top with a shortdough circle and freeze to set.

3. Unmold the bombes by running them under warm water. Return to the freezer until ready to spray.

4. Spray the bombes with the warm spraying mixture using a Wagner airless paint sprayer. Keep them in the freezer until ready to serve.

5. Place each bombe on a chocolate gear. Garnish with a clock tuile and a pulled sugar rod.

The wheel is white chocolate with a light spray of green cocoa butter. You can color cocoa butter with any kind of coloring agent, but Pfeiffer uses an oil-based powder. Pfeiffer always adds a touch of yellow to any chocolate or sugar that he is coloring, except when his object color is blue or white. "The yellow makes the finished color warmer, less harsh," he says, "and it also gives the sensation of light going through the piece."

To make the numeral "3": make a syrup by boiling three parts sugar to one part water. Pour into a pan, cover with plastic and cool overnight. Then pipe the numeral in Sweetex Copper (or another high-ratio shortening) onto a Silpat; sprinkle it with sugar, remove the excess, and freeze it. Take the cooled syrup, carefully skim off any sugar crystals on the surface, and place the number on the surface, face side down.

Refrigerate for 24 to 36 hours, until you have a thin coat of sugar. Much of the aesthetic lies in the thin nature of the form. Put the number in a warm spot (not an oven)—100 degrees—and the Sweetex will melt out.

1. Preheat oven to 350°F (180°C). In a mixer using the paddle attachment, cream together the butter, sugar, and vanilla bean seeds until light. Add half the egg whites, then half the flour and repeat with the remaining egg whites and flour. Mix just until combined.

2. Pass the cocoa paste through a clock-face silkscreen onto a sheet pan lined with a silicone baking mat. Let set.

3. Spread the tuile batter thinly through a clock-shape stencil on top of each clock face. Bake for 8 to 10 minutes or just until golden.

CHOCOLATE ICE CREAM			
	34 liq oz	1 lt	whole milk (3.6%)
	.7 liq oz	20 ml	heavy cream (35%)
	4.3 oz	121 g	granulated sugar
	2.3 oz	64 oz	inverted sugar
	2 oz	58 g	nonfat milk powder
	7.8 oz	220 g	DGF 64% bittersweet chocolate
	1.8 oz	50 g	DGF cocoa paste
	1.7 oz	48 g	egg yolks
	1 tsp	4 g	Sevarome ice cream stabilizer
	1 tsp	5 g	Sevarome monostearate

1. In a saucepan combine milk, cream, sugar, inverted sugar, and milk powder; place over high heat. At the same time, melt the chocolate and cocoa paste separately. When the milk mixture reaches 140°F (60°C) add the melted chocolate and cocoa paste, egg yolks, stabilizer, and monostearate. Cook gently, stirring, until the mixture reaches 185°F (85°C).

2. Strain the mixture over an ice bath and cool to 40°F (4°C), stirring occasionally. Refrigerate for at least 4 hours.

3. Process in an ice cream machine according to the manufacturer's instructions.

RASPBERRY COULIS			
	5.3 oz	150 g	raspberry purée (10% sugar)
	1.8 oz	50 g	inverted sugar
	.1 oz	4 g	gelatin sheets
	1.8 oz	50 g	dextrose
	.8 liq oz	24 ml	framboise d'Alsace

1. Combine the purée and inverted sugar and blend until smooth. Bloom the gelatin in cold water. Slightly warm 3.5 oz (100 g) of the purée and melt the gelatin in it. Temper into the remaining purée. Add the dextrose and liqueur. Cover tightly and chill until set.

2. When ready to line the bombes, warm the coulis very slightly.

VANILLA PARFAIT			
	6.4 oz	181 g	granulated sugar
	1.7 liq oz	50 ml	water
	7	7	Tahitian vanilla beans
	4.7 oz	132 g	egg yolks
	.4 oz	12.5 g	egg whites
	1 pt	473 ml	heavy cream (35%), whipped to soft peaks

> *"Chocolate is a lot more structurally sound than most people realize," says Donald Wressell. "When you mold the cone, you have to physically throw the chocolate out of the mold so that it becomes as thin as paper toward the top. This is not just for stability, though. When the diner applies a fork and just touches the top of the cone, it breaks away in pieces instead of toppling over into the sauce and ruining her evening gown."*
>
> *To unmold chocolate more easily, advises Chef Wressell, let it cool to room temperature, about an hour. Then put it in the refrigerator for ten minutes. It should pop out easily.*

GIANDUJA BAVARIAN

16 liq oz	473 ml	milk
8 oz	227 g	gianduja chocolate, finely chopped
.24 oz	6.7 g	gelatin sheets, softened in cold water
2 oz	57 g	praline paste
2 liq oz	59 ml	hazelnut-flavored liqueur, such as Frangelico
16 liq oz	473 ml	heavy cream, whipped to soft peaks

1. In a large saucepan, bring the milk to a boil. Reduce the heat and add the chocolate, drained gelatin, and praline paste. Stir until the chocolate and gelatin are melted and the mixture is smooth. Remove the pan from the heat and stir in the liqueur. Let cool to room temperature.

2. Fold the whipped cream into the chocolate mixture and pour into the prepared cones. Chill for at least 1 hour.

MANJARI ICE CREAM

9.75 oz	276 g	egg yolks
16 liq oz	473 ml	milk
16 liq oz	47 ml	heavy cream
9 oz	255 g	granulated sugar
.5 tsp	3.4 g	salt
1	1	vanilla bean, split and scraped
13 oz	369 g	Valrhona Manjari chocolate, finely chopped

1. In a medium bowl, whisk the yolks until smooth.

2. In a saucepan, bring the milk, cream, sugar, and salt to a boil. Temper the yolks with the cream mixture. Return to the saucepan and cook to the custard stage.

3. Place the chopped chocolate in a large bowl and strain the custard over the chocolate, discarding the vanilla bean. Stir until the chocolate is completely melted and the mixture is smooth.

4. Cool and chill.

5. Process in an ice cream machine according to the manufacturer's instructions.

BURNT ORANGE SAUCE

24 liq oz	710 ml	fresh orange juice
1.5 Tbs	18 g	tapioca starch
3 oz	85 g	granulated sugar
1.5	1.5	vanilla beans, split and scraped

1. In a saucepan, whisk together the orange juice and tapioca starch. Bring to a boil; lower the heat and keep the mixture warm.

2. In a heavy-bottom saucepan, cook the sugar and vanilla bean seeds to a dark caramel color.

3. Slowly add the warmed orange juice mixture to the caramel, stirring constantly, until the caramel is completely dissolved. Bring to a boil and boil for 2 minutes. Remove from heat.

4. Strain and chill.

HONEY "ECLIPSE" WAFER

7.5 oz	213 g	unsalted butter, softened
12 oz	340 g	confectioners' sugar
1/4 tsp	1.7 g	salt
1.5 oz	43 g	honey
10.5 oz	298 g	all-purpose flour, divided
7.5 oz	213 g	egg whites

1. In a mixer fitted with a paddle attachment, cream the butter with confectioners' sugar, salt, and honey.

2. On low speed, add half the flour and all the egg whites and mix until smooth. Add the remaining flour and continue mixing until the batter is well-blended. Chill for at least 2 hours.

3. Preheat the oven to 350°F (177°C). Line a sheet pan with parchment paper or a silicone baking mat. Cut an oval stencil whose major axis is 6" (15.2 cm) and whose minor axis is 3.75" (9.5 cm).

4. Place the stencil on the prepared sheet pan and spread a thin layer of batter over it. Repeat to make 14 wafers.

5. When the tuiles are half-baked (the dough will be pale but set), about 5 to 6 minutes, remove the sheet from the oven. Cut out the inside of each wafer with an oval cutter, leaving a 5/8" (1.6 cm) border. Return the "eclipse" rings to the oven and continue to bake until golden, about 5 to 6 minutes longer.

6. Remove wafers from the pan and bend each over a bowl to give it a slight curve. Let cool.

SESAME SEED WAFERS

4.5 oz	128 g	unsalted butter
4.5 oz	128 g	granulated sugar
1.5 oz	43 g	glucose
1.5 liq oz	44 ml	milk
8 oz	227 g	sesame seeds
2 oz	57 g	poppy seeds

1. In a medium saucepan, melt together the butter, sugar, and glucose.

2. Remove the pan from the heat and stir in the sesame and poppy seeds.

3. Chill for at least one hour.

4. Preheat the oven to 325°F (163°C). Line a sheet pan with a silicone baking mat.

5. Remove the sesame mixture from the refrigerator. Take 1/4 tsp of the mixture, form it into a ball with the palms of your hands, and place on the prepared pan. Continue forming the balls of mixture, placing them about 2" (5 cm) apart on the pan. (As these wafers are *extremely* fragile when baked, make more than needed.) Bake for 8 to 10 minutes, until toasted. Let cool completely.

6. With a small spatula, carefully transfer the wafers to a parchment-lined pan and reserve.

ASSEMBLY
Strawberry slices

1. Remove a dessert plate with the attached Bavarian-filled cones from the refrigerator.

2. Spoon 2 to 3 Tbs (30 to 45 ml) of the burnt-orange sauce around the tip of the cone to create a "pool" of sauce about 4 to 5" (10.2 to 12.7 cm) in diameter.

3. Place a small scoop (#60) of Manjari ice cream, three slices of strawberry, and two sesame-seed wafers on the Bavarian cream. Arrange an "eclipse" wafer on top of the cone. Repeat with the remaining plates.

MILK CHOCOLATE–GINGER MOUSSE WITH LIQUID CHOCOLATE CENTER

NORMAN LOVE

Corporate Pastry Chef, *Ritz-Carlton Hotel Company, Naples, Florida.*

Part of the inspiration for this dessert was the image of the cone and the sphere, but, says Norman Love, a further inspiration was the almond biscuit. "I attended a school at Valrhona in France, and one of the biscuits they taught was this one," he says. "It is primarily used with frozen desserts because it is moist and always stays very soft in the freezer. You're able to put crushed nuts or candied fruits or chocolate on the surface that will help accent the flavor of the dessert. Here, to accent the ginger and chocolate, I used pistachios and pine nuts."

YIELD: 20 SERVINGS

Special Equipment:
Twenty 2" (5 cm) PVC molds (2 1/2" (6.3 cm) high)
Forty Cocoa Barry 1" (2.5 cm) polycarbonate demi-sphere molds
Plastic cone molds, 2 3/4" base and 4 1/4" high (6.9 cm x 10.8 cm)

BISCUIT ALMANDE MOELLEUX			
	2.1 oz	*60 g*	*pine nuts, roasted*
	2.1 oz	*60 g*	*pistachio nuts, roasted*
	3.9 oz	*110 g*	*confectioners' sugar*
	3.9 oz	*110 g*	*almond powder*
	1.8 oz	*50 g*	*all-purpose flour*
	.9 oz	*25 g*	*heavy cream*
	10.6 oz	*302 g*	*egg whites, divided*
	4.4 oz	*125 g*	*granulated sugar*
	1 oz	*30 g*	*bittersweet chocolate, finely chopped*

1. Preheat the oven to 400°F (205°C) and line a sheet pan with a silicone baking mat.

2. In a food processor, coarsely grind the pine nuts and pistachio nuts and set aside.

3. Sift the confectioners' sugar and the almond powder into a bowl. Gently whisk in the flour until combined. Whisk in the cream and 2.6 oz (75 g) of the egg whites.

4. In a mixer fitted with a whisk attachment, begin whipping the remaining 8 oz (227 g) of egg whites. Gradually add the granulated sugar, beating until stiff peaks form. Fold in the almond mixture in two batches. Spread the batter evenly over the prepared baking mat. Sprinkle the nuts and chocolate over evenly and bake until set, about 7 minutes. Cool completely.

5. Cut out 1" (2.5 cm) wide strips of the biscuit to fit the interior of the PVC molds. Line the molds with the strips, nut-studded side against the mold.

PUR CARAIBE CHOCOLATE SPONGE			
	6.3 oz	180 g	Valrhona Pur Caraibe chocolate, chopped
	3 oz	85 g	unsalted butter, melted
	6.3 oz	180 g	egg whites
	1.8 oz	50 g	granulated sugar
	2.5 oz	70 g	egg yolks

1. Preheat the oven to 350°F (175°C) and line a half-sheet pan with a silicone baking mat.

2. Melt the chocolate with the butter to approximately 110°F (43°C)

3. In a mixer fitted with the whisk attachment, beat the egg whites with the sugar to stiff peaks. Gently whisk in the egg yolks, then fold in the chocolate mixture. Scrape the batter into a pastry bag fitted with a medium plain tip. Pipe the batter into 1 1/2" (3.8 cm) discs, and bake until set, about 10 minutes. Cool.

4. Place the chocolate sponge discs in the bottom of each of the lined PVC molds.

CHOCOLATE SAUCE			
	1 qt	946 ml	water
	9 oz	255 g	corn syrup
	17 oz	482 g	granulated sugar
	6 oz	170 g	cocoa powder
	1 lb	454 g	Valrhona Pur Caraibe chocolate, chopped

1. In a saucepan, combine the water, corn syrup, and sugar. Bring the mixture to a boil. Whisk in the cocoa powder and return the mixture to a boil, whisking until smooth.

2. Remove the pan from the heat and add the chocolate, stirring until smooth.

3. Line a half hotel pan with plastic wrap. Scrape the sauce into the pan. Freeze the sauce for several hours, until set.

4. Using a 3/4" (1.9 cm) round cutter, cut out 20 rounds of the frozen sauce. Return the rounds to the freezer until ready to assemble the dessert.

MILK CHOCOLATE-GINGER MOUSSE			
	4.4 oz	125 g	granulated sugar
	2 liq oz	59 ml	water
	1.8 oz	50 g	fresh ginger, finely chopped
	5.3 oz	150 g	egg yolks
	17.6 oz	500 g	Valrhona Javara milk chocolate
	3 sheets	7.5 g	gelatin leaves, bloomed
	33.8 liq oz	1 lt	heavy cream, whipped to soft peaks

1. In a saucepan, bring the sugar and water to a boil. Remove the pan from the heat and add the ginger. Allow the ginger to infuse in the syrup for at least 30 minutes.

2. Strain the syrup and return to the saucepan. Cook the syrup to 250°F (121°C).

3. Meanwhile, in a mixer fitted with a whisk attachment, begin beating the egg yolks. Gradually add the hot syrup in a thin stream to the beating yolks. Beat the mixture at medium speed until completely cool.

4. Melt the milk chocolate to 104°F (40°C); set aside.

5. Drain the gelatin and, in a small saucepan, heat on low until dissolved.

6. Fold half of the cream into the chocolate. Fold in the egg yolk mixture and gelatin. Fold in the remaining cream. Transfer the mousse to a pastry bag fitted with a medium plain tip.

7. Pipe the mousse into the prepared molds, filling them halfway. Place one of the frozen chocolate sauce discs in the center of each mold. Pipe more mousse on top, filling the molds completely and smoothing the top with a spatula. Freeze the molds for a few hours, until set.

SPHERICAL BASES	8 oz	227 g	cocoa butter
	as needed	as needed	fat-soluble food coloring (red, blue, and violet)*
	8 oz	227 g	white chocolate, tempered

*Note. Fat-soluble food coloring is available from Gourmand, Herndon, VA, (800) 627-7272.

1. Melt the cocoa butter and add a small amount of each color of the food coloring, until the mixture turns burgundy red. Using your finger, spread some of the mixture into the demi-sphere molds, coating them so that some areas are darker than others. Let the molds set for 5 minutes (see photos below).

2. Pour the tempered white chocolate into the prepared molds, filling them. Tap the molds sharply on a table to remove the air bubbles. Turn the molds upside down over a rack-covered bowl and tap to allow the excess chocolate to drip into the bowl. Using a dough scraper, remove the excess chocolate from the top of the molds and place the molds upside down on a parchment-lined sheet pan. Allow the molds to set completely.

3. Remove the demi-spheres from the molds. Heat a half-sheet pan in the oven until hot. Remove the pan and place it on a flat surface. Touch one of the chocolate demi-spheres to the hot sheet pan for less than 1 second. Immediately attach another chocolate demi-sphere to the first demi-sphere, creating a sealed sphere.

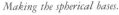
Making the spherical bases.

CHOCOLATE CONES	1.5 lbs	680 g	bittersweet chocolate, tempered

1. Ladle about 3 oz (85 g) of the melted chocolate into each cone. Turn the cones upside down and allow the excess chocolate to drip out. Allow to set.

2. Repeat with another layer of chocolate. Allow the cones to set completely.

CHOCOLATE DISCS	1 lb	454 g	bittersweet chocolate, tempered

1. Place a silicone baking mat on a flat work surface, with the textured side up. Pour the tempered chocolate onto the mat and, using a palette knife, spread it into a very thin and even layer. Allow the chocolate to set for a few minutes.

2. Using a 3" (7.6 cm) round cutter, cut out 20 discs from the chocolate; allow them to set completely.

CHOCOLATE GLAZE	1 qt	1 lt	milk
	15.8 oz	450 g	unsalted butter, cubed
	15.8 oz	450 g	granulated sugar
	8.8 oz	250 g	alkalized cocoa powder, sifted
	26.4 oz	750 g	bittersweet chocolate couverture, chopped
	8.8 oz	250 g	pâte à glacé, chopped

1. In a saucepan, whisk together the milk, butter, sugar, and cocoa powder over medium heat; bring this to a boil.

2. Add the couverture and pâte à glacé and whisk until smooth. Cool the glaze to about 85°F (29°C).

3. Remove the mousse molds from the freezer and, without unmolding them, spread a thin layer of the glaze over each dessert. Place the molds in the refrigerator until ready to serve.

CHOCOLATE TRIANGLES	1 lb	454 g	milk chocolate couverture, tempered
	1 lb	454 g	bittersweet chocolate couverture, tempered

1. Make two triangular stencils out of cardboard using the drawing on the following page as a guide, making one 5 x 2 1/2 x 4 1/2" (12.7 x 6.3 x 11.4 cm) and the other 3 1/2 x 1 1/2 x 3" (8.8 x 3.8 x 7.6 cm). Place 2 silicone baking mats on a flat work surface, with the textured sides up. Pour some of the tempered milk chocolate onto one of the mats and, using a palette knife, spread it into a thin, even layer. Allow the chocolate to set for a few minutes.

2. Repeat the procedure with the bittersweet couverture.

3. Using the stencils as a guide, cut out several triangles from each of the chocolates using an X-acto knife. Set the triangles aside until ready to garnish the dessert.

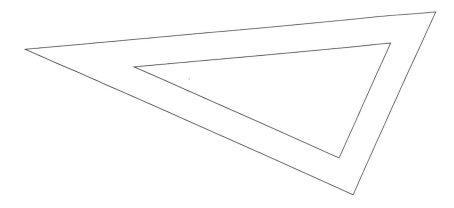

ASSEMBLY   *Tempered bittersweet chocolate couverture*
            Chocolate sauce

1. Place a dot of tempered couverture in the center of a dessert plate. Glue one of the spheres to the plate. Allow to set.

2. Heat a small plain writing tip and poke a small hole in the top of the sphere. Dip the tip of one of the chocolate cones in the tempered couverture and place in the hole. Allow it to set.

3. Place one of the chocolate discs on top of the cone. Unmold one of the glazed desserts and place it on top of the disc.

4. Dip the tip of two of the larger triangles into the chocolate and attach them to the disc, as in the photograph. Stick two of the smaller triangles into the top of the dessert. Place a few graduated drops of chocolate sauce on the plate. Repeat with the remaining plates.

HOT LIPS

MARTIN HOWARD

Pastry Chef, *Rainbow!*, New York.

White chocolate mousse covered in raspberry sauce is placed on a chocolate chip cookie that has been glazed with chocolate. More white chocolate mousse and a mixed berry compote are placed underneath. To complete this provocative image are raspberry sauce, apricot sauce, and white chocolate flames submerged in chocolate cups filled with Grand Marnier ganache. The cookie should ideally be crunchy on the outside, slightly soft on the inside.

YIELD: 15 SERVINGS

CHOCOLATE CHIP COOKIES			
7.5 oz	213 g	cake flour
1 tsp	5 g	baking soda
8 oz	227 g	unsalted butter, softened
4 oz	113 g	light brown sugar
3.5 oz	99 g	granulated sugar
1.75 oz	50 g	eggs
.5 tsp	2 g	salt
1 tsp	5 ml	vanilla extract
8 oz	227 g	large-size chocolate chips

1. Preheat the oven to 325°F (163°C). Line a sheet pan with parchment paper.

2. In a bowl, sift together the cake flour and baking soda.

3. In a mixer fitted with a paddle attachment, beat the butter until creamy. Gradually add the light brown and granulated sugars and continue to beat until smooth. Add the eggs, salt, and vanilla extract; beat until blended. On low speed add the dry ingredients. Mix in the chocolate chips.

4. Using a #24 scoop, which is a scant 2 oz (57 g) of dough, drop the dough onto the prepared pan and bake for 15 to 18 minutes, until golden. (The edges of the cookies will be set, but the centers will still be soft.) Let the cookies rest on the pan for 5 minutes, then transfer to a rack to cool completely.

CHOCOLATE GLAZE			
8 oz	227 g	bittersweet chocolate, chopped
8 liq oz	237 ml	heavy cream
4 liq oz	118 ml	corn syrup

1. Place the chopped chocolate in a bowl.

2. In a saucepan bring the heavy cream and corn syrup to a boil.

3. Pour the hot cream mixture over the chocolate and stir until the chocolate is melted and the sauce is smooth.

WHITE CHOCOLATE MOUSSE			
3.75 oz	*106 g*	*egg yolks*
2.5 oz	*71 g*	*granulated sugar*
4 liq oz	*118 ml*	*dry white wine*
14 oz	*397 g*	*white chocolate, melted*
32 liq oz	*946 ml*	*heavy cream*
2 tsp	*10 ml*	*vanilla extract*
2 Tbs	*30 ml*	*kirsch liqueur*

1. Line a sheet pan with parchment paper.

2. In a large bowl over simmering water, whisk together the egg yolks, granulated sugar, and white wine until light and thick. Whisk in the melted chocolate.

3. In a mixer fitted with the whisk attachment, combine the heavy cream, vanilla extract, and kirsch. Whip to soft peaks. Fold into the yolk-chocolate mixture. Chill the mousse until firm.

4. Fill a pastry bag fitted with a plain tip (Ateco #6) with the mousse and pipe out 15 pairs of lips (about 3 1/2"/8.8 cm wide) onto the prepared pan. With the remaining mousse, pipe out 15 mounds of mousse 1" (2.5 cm) diameter x 1 3/4" (4.4 cm) high and pipe out 15 mounds of mousse 1 1/4" (3.1 cm) diameter x 1 1/2" (3.8 cm) high. Freeze the mousse lips and mounds.

MIXED BERRY SALAD			
44 oz	*1.2 kg*	*mixed berries, such as strawberries, raspberries, and cherries*
2 oz	*57 g*	*granulated sugar*
1 liq oz	*30 ml*	*Grand Marnier*

1. Roughly chop the berries.

2. Place the berries, granulated sugar, and Grand Marnier in a large bowl and toss to combine.

RASPBERRY SAUCE			
36 oz	*1 kg*	*fresh raspberries*
12 oz	*340 g*	*granulated sugar*
1/2	*1/2*	*whole lemon*

1. In a medium saucepan, combine the raspberries, granulated sugar, and lemon half. Bring the mixture to a boil; reduce the heat and simmer until thickened, about 10 minutes.

2. Remove the lemon. Strain through a chinois to extract the seeds and chill.

APRICOT SAUCE			
18 oz	*510 g*	*apricot purée*
4 oz	*113 g*	*granulated sugar*

In a medium saucepan, combine the apricot purée and sugar; bring to a boil. Reduce the heat and simmer for 10 minutes. Chill.

GANACHE CUPS	16 oz	454 g	bittersweet chocolate, finely chopped
	12 liq oz	355 ml	heavy cream
	2 oz	57 g	granulated sugar
	2 oz	57 g	unsalted butter
	1 liq oz	30 ml	Grand Marnier liqueur
	75	75	small chocolate cups*

*Note. Small chocolate cups are available from Patisfrance, (800) PASTRY-1.

1. Place the chopped chocolate in a bowl.

2. In a saucepan, bring the heavy cream, granulated sugar, and butter to a boil.

3. Pour the hot cream mixture over the chocolate. Stir until the chocolate is melted and the mixture is smooth. Add the Grand Marnier.

4. Spoon about 2 teaspoons of the ganache into each chocolate cup.

| WHITE CHOCOLATE FLAMES | 12 oz | 340 g | white chocolate, tempered |

Spread a thin layer of the chocolate onto the parchment. When set, cut into 75 curved triangular shapes, about 3/4 x 5 1/2" (1.9 x 14 cm).

ASSEMBLY

1. Place the chocolate chip cookies on a rack set over a sheet pan so that the bottom of each cookie is facing up. Pour the chocolate glaze over the cookies and drain on the rack until set.

2. Remove 1 pair of lips, 2 large mounds of mousse, and 2 small mounds of mousse from the freezer. Paint the lips with raspberry sauce and place on the center of a glazed cookie.

3. Place four mounds of mousse near the center of the dessert plate, so that the larger ones are behind the smaller ones. These are arranged so that the cookie will be propped up at an angle. Spoon about 1/3 cup of the berry salad in the center of the mousse. Place the cookie on top of the berries.

4. Arrange 5 white chocolate flames around the cookie. Garnish the plate with apricot and raspberry sauces in a flame motif.

CHOCOLATE RASPBERRY CAKE

EN-MING HSU

Assistant Pastry Chef, *Ritz-Carlton Hotel, Chicago.*

"I was trying to do something classic—chocolate and raspberry, which we know go well together—with some crunch and smooth elements," says En-Ming Hsu. The chocolate cream that encases the sablée and raspberries is not quite a mousse and not quite a ganache—based on an anglaise, it has a very silky, custard-like texture. Chocolate apricot glaze covers all, and the raspberries used as garnish are filled with mascarpone.

YIELD: 12 SERVINGS

Special Equipment:
Twelve ring molds, 2.3" (6 cm) diameter x 1.6" (4 cm) high
Two 9" (22.8 cm) cake rings

VANILLA SABLÉE

2.2 oz	*65 g*	*unsalted butter*
1.1 oz	*30 g*	*confectioners' sugar*
2	*2*	*large egg yolks, hard boiled*
1	*1*	*vanilla bean, split and scraped*
3 oz	*85 g*	*cake flour*
1/8 tsp	*.5 g*	*baking powder*

1. Preheat oven to 325°F (165°C). In a mixer fitted with a paddle attachment, beat the butter and sugar untl light and fluffy. Pass the egg yolks through a tamis and add it to the butter along with the vanilla bean seeds. Sift together the flour and baking powder and add it to the mixture. Mix just until incorporated. Form the dough into a disc, wrap it in plastic, and refrigerate overnight.

2. On a lightly floured surface roll the dough to a 1/8" (3 mm) thickness. Dock and cut the dough into 2" (5 cm) rounds. Place on a parchment-lined sheet pan and bake for 15 to 20 minutes or until pale golden in color. Cool completely.

CHOCOLATE CREAM

14 liq oz	*400 ml*	*heavy cream*
14 liq oz	*400 ml*	*whole milk*
5.3 oz	*150 g*	*granulated sugar, divided*
4.6 oz	*130 g*	*egg yolks*
19.8 oz	*560 g*	*Valrhona Pur Caraibe chocolate, chopped*

1. In a saucepan combine the cream, milk, and 2.7 oz (75 g) of the sugar and bring to a boil. Whisk together the egg yolks with the remaining 2.7 oz (75 g) of the sugar. Temper the yolks into the milk mixture and cook gently, stirring, until the mixture coats the back of a wooden spoon.

2. Strain the cream into a bowl containing the chopped chocolate. Whisk until the chocolate is completely melted and incorporated with the cream. Cover the surface with plastic wrap and chill until it is firm enough to pipe.

CHOCOLATE SOUFFLÉ BISCUIT

3.5 oz	100 g	*Valrhona Pur Caraibe chocolate*
.9 oz	25 g	*cocoa paste*
6.3 oz	180 g	*egg yolks*
5.5 oz	155 g	*granulated sugar, divided*
8 oz	225 g	*egg whites*

1. Preheat oven to 350°F (175°C). Melt the chocolate and cocoa paste together over a double boiler. Keep the melted chocolate in a warm spot to hold it at about 110°F (43°C).

2. In a mixer, whip the egg yolks with 2 oz (55 g) of the sugar until very light and pale. Whip the egg whites with the remaining 3.5 oz (100 g) of sugar to a stiff meringue. Fold the melted chocolate into the yolks, then fold in the meringue. Evenly divide the batter into two 9" (22.8 cm) cake rings on a parchment-lined sheet pan. Bake for 15 to 20 minutes or until a cake tester comes out clean. Cool completely and freeze until firm enough to cut.

MIRROR GLAZE

13.5 liq oz	400 ml	*heavy cream*
16.2 oz	460 g	*Valrhona Pur Caraibe chocolate, chopped*
1.6 oz	45 g	*unsalted butter, softened*
3.2 oz	90 g	*corn syrup*

1. In a saucepan bring the cream to a boil and pour it into a bowl containing the chocolate. Whisk until the chocolate is thoroughly dissolved and let it cool to room temperature.

2. Whisk in the butter and corn syrup until fully incorporated.

RASPBERRY FILLING

1 pt	1 pt	*fresh raspberries*
1 liq oz	30 ml	*raspberry purée, 10% sugar*
1 liq oz	30 ml	*simple syrup*
		Lemon juice to taste

Combine all the ingredients, tossing gently, so as not to damage the raspberries. Add a few drops of lemon juice if desired.

RASPBERRY COULIS

8 oz	227 g	*fresh ripe raspberries*
1 oz	28 g	*granulated sugar*
2 oz	57 g	*dextrose*

Combine all ingredients in a food processor and purée. Pass the mixture through a chinois.

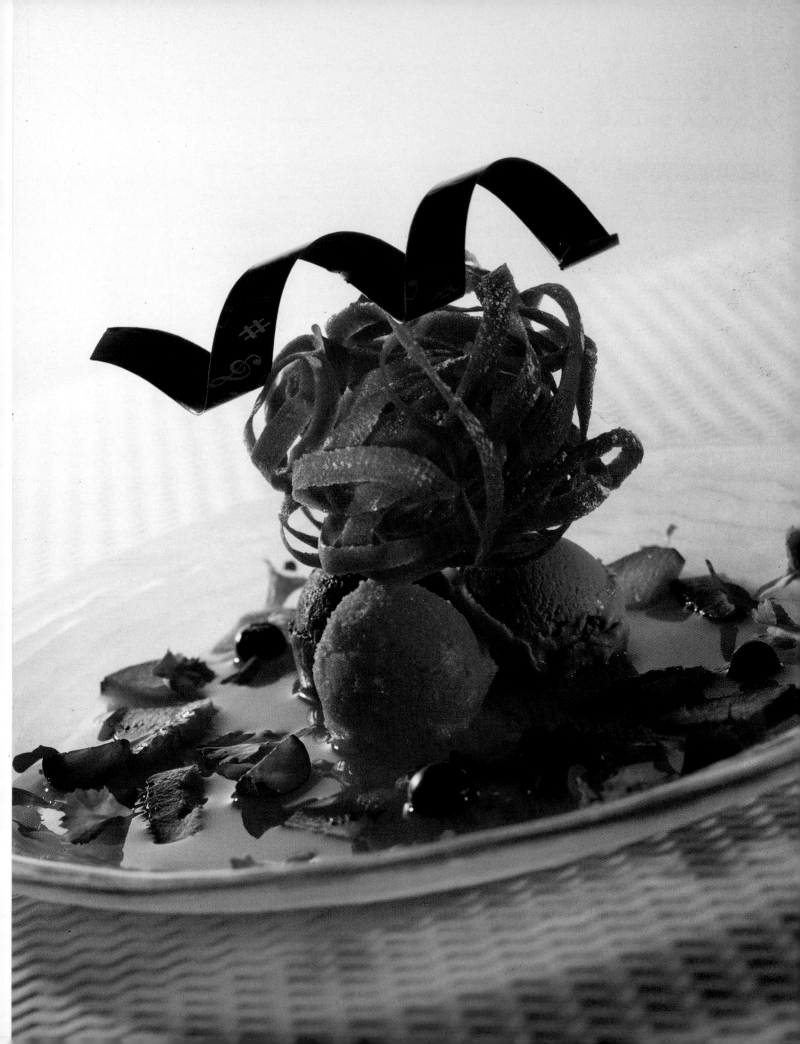

CHOCOLATE ICE CREAM			
54 liq oz	1.6 lt	milk
1 liq oz	30 ml	heavy cream
6.5 oz	184 g	granulated sugar, divided
3 oz	85 g	trimoline
3 oz	85 g	nonfat milk powder
12 oz	340 g	Valrhona Caraque bittersweet chocolate
3 oz	85 g	Valrhona cocoa paste
3 oz	85 g	egg yolks
1 tsp	5 g	Sevarome ice cream stabilizer

1. In a saucepan, combine the milk, heavy cream, 6 oz (170 g) of the sugar, trimoline, and milk powder; cook over medium heat, just until warm.

2. Meanwhile, melt the bittersweet chocolate and cocoa paste separately and then whisk together.

3. Add some of the warm milk mixture to the chocolate mixture and whisk until smooth. Add this mixture to the remaining milk mixture and whisk to combine.

4. In a bowl, whisk together the yolks, ice cream stabilizer, and the remaining .5 oz (14 g) of sugar; add this to the chocolate mixture. Stirring constantly with a rubber spatula, cook to 185°F (85°C). Strain the mixture and cool over an ice bath to 40°F (4°C). Cover the mixture and chill overnight, to allow the flavors to mature.

5. Process the mixture in an ice cream machine according to the manufacturer's instructions.

TANGERINE-LEMONGRASS SORBET			
1 pt	473 ml	simple syrup (60%)
2 stalks	2 stalks	lemongrass, chopped
48 liq oz	1.4 lt	tangerine juice
2 tsp	10 g	sorbet stabilizer
1 oz	28 g	granulated sugar

1. In a saucepan, combine the simple syrup and lemongrass. Bring the mixture to a boil, remove from the heat, cover, and allow to infuse for 2 hours. Strain and chill for several hours.

2. Combine the syrup and the tangerine juice. In a separate bowl, combine the sorbet stabilizer and the sugar. Add this to the syrup mixture and whisk until well combined. Process the mixture in an ice cream machine according to the manufacturer's instructions.

CITRUS SAUCE			
32 liq oz	946 ml	fresh orange juice, strained
6 oz	170 g	orange blossom honey
6 oz	170 g	granulated sugar
2 Tbs	30 ml	cold water
2 tsp	10 g	arrowroot
2 liq oz	59 ml	Grand Marnier liqueur

1. In a saucepan, combine the orange juice, honey, and sugar; bring mixture to just under a boil. Remove from the heat.

2. In a small container, combine the water and arrowroot. Add the mixture to the saucepan; and cook until just slightly thickened. Stir in the liqueur. Strain the sauce and chill.

VANILLA SALAD	1 lb 3 oz	539 g	granulated sugar
	1 lb 3 oz	539 g	bread flour
	4	4	Tahitian vanilla beans, split and scraped
	1 lb 3 oz	539 g	unsalted butter
	12 oz	340 g	egg whites, warmed slightly

1. In a bowl, combine the sugar and the flour.

2. In a mixer fitted with the paddle attachment, combine the vanilla bean seeds and butter; mix until well blended. Pass the butter through a fine sieve and melt.

3. Whisk the egg whites into sugar-flour mixture. Whisk in the melted butter. Pour the mixture into plastic squeeze bottles and chill for several hours.

4. Line a sheet pan with a silicone baking mat and preheat the oven to 350°F (175°C). Pipe the batter onto the baking mat in four spiral patterns. Pipe the spirals from the center out, leaving about 1/2" (1.27 cm) between each line. Bake until golden brown, about 8 minutes. Remove the pan from the oven and quickly but gently pull each spiral off the mat and toss it in your hands until a round ball or "salad" has formed. Place in a tightly covered container that has a drying agent in it (such as limestone). Repeat with the remaining batter to form a total of 16 "salads."

ASSEMBLY
Confectioners' sugar
Assorted diced tropical fruit
Assorted berries
Edible flower petals
Chocolate spiral garnish

1. Place a scoop of the chocolate ice cream, raspberry-mascarpone ice cream, and tangerine-lemongrass sorbet in a triangular pattern in the center of a dessert plate. Thinly cover the rest of the plate with the citrus sauce.

2. Gently place a vanilla salad round on top of the scoops. Dust the salad with confectioners' sugar.

3. Garnish the sauce with a mixture of diced tropical fruits, berries, and edible flower petals. Finish the plate with a chocolate spiral.

BLACKBERRY—RASPBERRY "SODA"

ERIC PEREZ

Executive Pastry Chef, *Ritz-Carlton, Tyson's Corners, Virginia.*

Chef Perez has devised a sleek, attention-getting way to present sorbets: a blackberry tuile encloses lemon sherbet and raspberry sorbet. The cone is served with berries, blackberry pâte de fruit, a blown sugar ball, and bubble sugar. The base of the cone is chocolate. With the dominant flavors of blackberry, raspberry, and lemon, this is a very tart but palate-pleasing dessert.

YIELD: 20 SERVINGS

BLACKBERRY PÂTE DE FRUIT			
.5 oz	14 g	pectin
30 oz	851 g	granulated sugar, divided
26.5 oz	751 g	blackberry purée
6.5 oz	184 g	glucose
.5 oz	14 g	citric acid

1. In a saucepan combine the pectin with 2.5 oz (71 g) of the sugar. Stir in the purée and bring the mixture to a boil. Add the remaining 27.5 oz (780 g) of the sugar and the glucose and cook to 221°F (105°C).

2. Remove the pan from the heat, add the citric acid, and pour onto a half-sheet pan lined with aluminum foil. Let cool completely and cut into 1" (2.5 cm) squares. Coat each square with granulated sugar.

BLACKBERRY TUILE			
28 oz	794 g	granulated sugar
7 oz	198 g	all-purpose flour, sifted
4 liq oz	118 ml	orange juice
5 oz	142 g	blackberry purée
10 oz	284 g	unsalted butter, melted

1. Preheat oven to 375°F (190°C). Place a sheet pan in the oven to warm. Combine the sugar and flour. Add the orange juice and purée. Mix in the melted butter.

2. Drop the batter onto a silicone baking mat using a 1.5 oz (44 ml) scoop as a measure. Spread the batter into a thin circle with an offset spatula. Transfer the baking mat to the warm sheet pan and return it to the oven. Bake for 8 to 10 minutes or just until the edges turn golden. Immediately flip each tuile over and roll it around a cone. Let set.

LEMON SHERBET			
1 qt	946 ml	whole milk
12 oz	340 g	granulated sugar
5	5	lemons, zest and juice

1. In a saucepan combine the milk, sugar, and lemon zest and bring the mixture to a boil. Strain it through a chinois over an ice bath and cool completely.

2. Process the sherbet base in an ice cream machine. Add the lemon juice while the machine is running.

RASPBERRY SORBET			
	6 oz	170 g	granulated sugar
	.75 tsp	2.5 g	sorbet stabilizer
	4 liq oz	118 ml	water
	3 oz	85 g	glucose
	1 qt	946 ml	raspberry purée

1. In a saucepan combine the sugar and stabilizer. Add the water and glucose and bring the mixture to a boil. Cool completely and refrigerate overnight.

2. Combine the syrup with the raspberry purée. Process in an ice cream machine according to the manufacturer's instructions.

CHOCOLATE CYLINDERS AND BASES			
	8 oz	227 g	cocoa butter
	A few drops		Chefmaster oil-based purple coloring
	1 lb	454 g	white chocolate, tempered

1. Melt the cocoa butter and add purple coloring to desired color. When the cocoa butter has cooled and thickened a bit (it may be necessary to temper it for a few seconds on a marble slab), spread it thinly on acetate right triangles 7" (17.8 cm) long x 1" (2.5 cm) high and acetate circles 3.5" (8.9 cm) in diameter. Let set completely.

2. Spread the white chocolate over the cocoa butter.

3. To make the cylinders, twist the acetate around a 2" (5 cm) diameter PVC pipe. Let set completely. For the bases, let the chocolate set and remove the acetate.

CHOCOLATE STRAWS			
	1 lb	454 g	cocoa butter
	A few drops		Chefmaster oil-based purple coloring
	1 lb	454 g	white chocolate, tempered

1. Melt the cocoa butter and add purple coloring to desired color. When the cocoa butter has cooled and thickened a bit (it may be necessary to temper it for a few seconds on a marble slab), spread it thinly on marble and drag a fine-tooth comb through it. Let set.

2. Spread a thin coat of white chocolate over the cocoa butter. When the chocolate has just started to set, use the metal blade of a bench scraper to form tight cigarettes.

ASSEMBLY	
	Bubble sugar
	Pulled-sugar straws
	Mint sprigs
	Assorted fresh berries

1. Heat the narrow end of each tuile cone with a torch to melt it slightly. Attach it to a chocolate base and let set completely.

2. Place a scoop of lemon sherbet in each cone and top it with a scoop of raspberry sorbet. Place a piece of bubble sugar in the sorbet. Add a chocolate straw, pulled-sugar straw, and mint sprig to each cone.

3. Place a chocolate cylinder on the plate and fill it with fresh berries. Add two pâte de fruit squares and a blown-sugar ball to each plate.

Making the chocolate cylinders (see above).

"I don't believe that art is self-expression. It is only interesting to yourself, keep it to yourself."

W. H. AUDEN

"Cauliflower is nothing but cabbage with a college education."

MARK TWAIN

C H A P T E R **T** W O

MODERNIZING THE CLASSICS

D. JEMAL EDWARDS

Pastry Chef
SoHo Sushi, New York.

BORN: September 1966,
Ankara, Turkey.
TRAINING/EXPERIENCE: Mirador
and the Cypress Club, Chicago;
Elka and Liberté, San Francisco;
Montrachet, Nobu, and
Maxim's, New York.

*"I'm really dedicated to what I'm
doing. It's basically 95 percent of
my life. That's a bad balance, I
know, to have that much of your life
be your job or your career. Perhaps
time spent doing other things could
be fulfilling as well. There are
other things I would like to do, but
can't. I'm doing what I need to be
doing right now. Maybe in five
years I'll rethink my priorities and
perspectives, but right now my prior-
ity is my career."*

KRISTA KERN

Pastry Chef, *Three Fish, Westerly,
Rhode Island.*

BORN: November 1966,
Toronto, Canada.
TRAINING/EXPERIENCE: The
Elms, Maine; Symphony Cafe,
New York; Bang, Greenwich,
Connecticut; Sullivan's, New
York.

*"I love intricate plates. I love play-
ing and making pastry fun. I'm
always thinking about it. Elizabeth
DeFranco, who was the chef at the
Elms, taught me to respect the ingredients I'm working with, and that
everything you work with and
everything you do is important. You
never take shortcuts. It's always better in the long run to do it correctly.
It's more of a feeling than a set of
rules she imparted to me, but wher-
ever I go, it's always with me."*

"In France they have a tendency to stick to the rules too much," observes Jacquy Pfeiffer of Ecole de Patisserie Francaise School in Chicago. "If you are overcreative, you'll get hit over the head by the old-timers. In America it is the opposite. You have maybe too many people creating too many things and forgetting the basics. But it's good to be creative. Even if there are nine bad ideas and one good, still that's one good idea."

It's an age-old tension, often characterized as the familiar, staid grandeur of classic works versus the passionate experimentation of the romantic. The Modernist movement in the arts, as we have seen, was all about toppling rules, outraging conservative sensibilities, venturing into the new.

So how does that translate into the pastry kitchen? Are there rules when it comes to creating quality pastry? If so, what are they? Who can successfully break the rules—old masters, confident in their abilities, or brash youngbloods, disdainful of all rules?

There is one rule that is often cited by pastry chefs as a viable, common-sense rule: the Three-Flavor Rule. "Some chefs play so much that the flavors get muddled. It gets too bizarre," says En-Ming Hsu of the Ritz-Carlton Chicago. "Stick to three flavors. Classic combinations. You always know what works from the basics. It's fairly foolproof."

"There are rules," admits Martin Howard, that perennial rule-breaker from Rainbow! in New York. "There are some that can be broken and some that can't. There are certain leavening techniques, other elements of the science of baking, that you cannot fool with."

But many of the rules of classic French training, which have solid historical footing, may not pertain anymore. "Because there was no refrigeration, they were limited as to what they could prepare and preserve," Richard Ruskell, pastry chef at the Phoenician in Phoenix, points out. "Hence you had a lot of things with marzipan because they were sitting out a long time. So there were rules."

That having been said, however, both Ruskell and Howard assert that there *are* no rules: "A lot of people don't want you to mess with the classics," says Howard, "but I believe that if you can make it better or more interesting, why not?" After further thought, Howard admits that he has one unshakable dessert rule: "Bigger is better."

"The only rule is your taste," says Ruskell. "Taste in a five senses sort of way, and taste in your sense of visual appeal."

Other chefs disagree, and with glee: "There are no rules, no boundaries," says Thomas Worhach of the Ocean Grand in Palm Beach, "and I think it's exciting, it's fun. Everyone has their own style. Some people will say that it should be this way or that way, but you can't speak for all the guests who come into your restaurant. All these people have different tastes also."

"I can't think of any rules," says Wayne Brachman of Mesa Grill in New York. "There are preferences, styles. I don't like to place things very specifically. I like to place things in haphazard ways, but that's not a rule. There is practical advice. For example, I've worked with people who need to hear: don't put sauce on the center of the plate if you're going to put a piece of cake on it. If you're a putz, you need that rule."

"There are no rules," agrees Philippe Laurier of Patisfrance. "If the balance is right, and the basic dessert is good, why not? Anything goes."

A sentiment only a Modernist could love—anything goes. But in the fine arts, there was an inevitable backlash to Modernism's freewheeling destruction of centuries of classic aesthetics. One of the most thoughtful essays in reaction to Modernism was written in 1984 by Suzi Gablik. In "Has Modernism Failed?" she points out that the "steady violation of expected continuities . . . is radically at odds with systemic wisdom and equilibrium.

So many metamorphoses and revolutions ...so many different values presented simultaneously, have finally done away with the frame of things—and destroyed any conviction that there are any limits to art at all..." Gablik writes. "Having removed any standards...we no longer know what rules we ought to follow, much less why we ought to follow them.... Only with hindsight can we now see that tradition and authority may be necessary, even to make a genuine avant garde possible, in order to provide something to revolt against."

Gablik cites a law of history that Heraclitus called enantiodromia: when one principle reaches the height of its power, it collapses into its opposite. "Artists are finding that the only way to make something new is to borrow from the past," writes Gablik. Modernism's "renunciations of so much that is crucial to human well-being—in the name of freedom and self-sufficiency—are what will have failed us."

So it is interesting that so many chefs in this book express the hope, as delineated in Chapter 1, that "Modernism" may mean a return to pure flavors, to simplicity. Enantiodromia anyone?

"It's important for a pastry chef to have a solid grounding in the basics," says Donald Wressell of the Four Seasons Beverly Hills, echoing what many other chefs in this volume stated. "Once you have that, it's okay to venture off and break the rules. I tend to assign new people to make cookies, cakes, chocolate mousse, ice cream bases, syrup, lemon curd, pastry cream. Once they master that, they can become part of the group that generates ideas."

"When you work with a lot of people, have them under your tutelage," says Stanton Ho of the Las Vegas Hilton, "you find that some break away and experiment on their own, which is okay. I encourage them to do that. But most come full circle. They come around to my way of doing things."

Throughout this book, of course, classic recipes are being exploited, as they are everywhere, every day. But with the desserts in this chapter the chefs have deliberately taken the major components of classic recipes and, by tinkering with the presentation, arrived at something new. Or, in some cases, they have taken major liberties with the classic recipe itself. They vividly demonstrate how imagination, daring, and affection can combine to create something new from the tried (sometimes trite) and true.

For her Rhubarb Strawberry Strudel, Krista Kern takes the classic strudel and shapes it vertically, using phyllo, which is an acceptable, fairly common substitute for traditional strudel dough. She only tinkers with the classic formula by providing some four garnishes, rather than the classic dollop of ice cream. Michael Hu lightens the classic Mont Blanc,

MARSHALL ROSENTHAL

Executive Pastry Chef
Trump Taj Mahal Hotel and Casino, Atlantic City, New Jersey.

BORN: September 1959, Baltimore, Maryland.
TRAINING/EXPERIENCE: various patisseries and bakeries, Baltimore area; Hyatt Hotels; Royal Sonesta, Boston; Renaissance Harborplace Hotel, Baltimore.

"Constantly steer your boat into the wind. Go for the challenge. From year to year I don't know what's next, but I know there will always be new challenges. You have to run your daily operation, but you also have to keep up with the profession—read, go to seminars and competitions, and always, always remain hands-on. There are times when I wonder, why am I trying so hard? But if you collect a check, you're accountable. As one of my mentors used to say to us: 'Shut up and work.'"

Yellow Pâte

1. In a mixer fitted with the paddle attachment, cream together the remaining 7 oz (198 g) of the butter and the remaining 7 oz (198 g) of the confectioners' sugar. Blend in the remaining 7 oz (198 g) of the egg whites. Blend in the remaining 7 oz (198 g) of flour and enough yellow food coloring to make it an egg yolk hue.

2. Line a baking sheet with a silicone baking mat. Cover the mat with a star stencil. Spread a thin, even layer of the yellow pâte over the stencil. Remove the stencil and freeze the pâte-covered sheet for about 1 hour.

JOCONDE

13.25 oz	*376 g*	*confectioners' sugar*
3.5 oz	*99 g*	*cake flour*
4 oz	*113 g*	*unsweetened cocoa powder*
13.25 oz	*376 g*	*almond flour*
17.5 oz	*496 g*	*whole eggs*
2.75 oz	*78 g*	*unsalted butter, melted*
11.5 oz	*326 g*	*egg whites*
1.75 oz	*50 g*	*granulated sugar*
as needed	*as needed*	*yellow food coloring as needed*

COCOA JOCONDE

1. Preheat oven to 375°F (130°C). In a bowl, sift together 6.6 oz (188 g) of the confectioners' sugar, 1.75 oz (50 g) of the cake flour, and the cocoa powder. Whisk in 6.6 oz (188 g) of the almond flour.

2. In a mixer with the paddle attachment, beat together 8.75 oz (248 g) of the eggs and 1.4 oz (39 g) of the butter at medium speed until combined. At low speed, add the dry ingredients and mix until combined.

3. In a mixer with the whisk attachment, beat 5.75 oz (163 g) of the egg whites with .87 oz (25 g) of the sugar to stiff peaks. Fold the egg whites into the batter. Spread the cocoa batter evenly over the yellow stenciled stars (it will be a thin layer). Bake for 6 to 8 minutes, until set. While still hot, flip the cake over and peel off the silicone baking mat. Cool completely.

4. Using the 2 3/4" (6.9 cm) triangle template, cut the cake into 48 triangles.

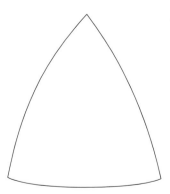

YELLOW JOCONDE

1. In a bowl, sift together the remaining 6.6 oz (188 g) of confectioners' sugar and the remaining 1.75 oz (50 g) of the cake flour. Whisk in the remaining 6.6 oz (188 g) of the almond flour.

1. Preheat oven to 350°F (175°C). Line a half-sheet pan with parchment paper.

2. In a mixer fitted with a paddle attachment, cream together the butter and confectioners' sugar. Add the eggs and mix until incorporated.

3. On low speed, add the almond and all-purpose flours to the creamed mixture and mix until combined.

4. Shape the dough into a disc and refrigerate for 1 hour.

5. Remove the dough from the refrigerator and roll out to 1/8" (.32 cm) thickness. Using a 3" (7.6 cm) round cutter, cut out 10 rounds of dough and place them on the prepared pan.

6. Bake for 10 to 12 minutes, until lightly browned. Cool on a rack.

| CRÈME FRAÎCHE FILLING | 8 oz | 227 g | crème fraîche |
| | 1 Tbs | 14 g | granulated sugar |

Whip the crème fraîche with the sugar to stiff peaks. Refrigerate until needed.

WARM RASPBERRY PUDDING	6 oz	170 g	whole milk ricotta cheese
	4 oz	113 g	granulated sugar, divided
	1.5 oz	43 g	egg yolks
	1 oz	28 g	all-purpose flour
	6 oz	170 g	egg whites
	5 oz	142 g	fresh raspberries

1. Preheat oven to 325°F (163°C).

2. In a bowl, combine the ricotta cheese, 2 oz (57 g) of the sugar, and the egg yolks. Whisk in the flour to make a smooth paste.

3. In a mixer fitted with a whisk attachment, whip the egg whites and sugar to soft peaks.

4. Fold the meringue into the cheese mixture. Fold in the raspberries.

5. Fill the buttered ramekins with the raspberry-cheese mixture to two-thirds full. Bake in a water bath for 25 to 30 minutes, until the pudding is set and golden brown.

RASPBERRY SORBET	18 oz	510 g	fresh raspberries
	4 liq oz	118 ml	water
	13 liq oz	384 ml	simple syrup

1. Purée the raspberries with the water in a food processor. Strain the mixture through a chinois to extract the seeds. Combine the raspberry purée with the simple syrup and chill.

2. Process in an ice cream machine according to the manufacturer's instructions.

SOUR CREAM ICE CREAM	16 liq oz	473 ml	half-and-half
	6 oz	170 g	granulated sugar
	4 oz	113 g	egg yolks
	1 lb	454 g	sour cream

1. In a large saucepan, combine the half-and-half and sugar, and bring to a boil.

2. In a bowl, temper the yolks with hot cream mixture. Return the mixture to the saucepan and whisk in the sour cream. Strain the mixture through a chinois and cool in ice bath. Chill.

3. Process in an ice cream machine according to the manufacturer's instructions.

ALMOND CAKE	7 oz	198 g	almond paste
	7 oz	198 g	sugar
	7 oz	198 g	butter, softened
	7 oz	198 g	eggs
	3 oz	85 g	cake flour

1. Preheat oven to 325°F (163°C). Line 2 half-sheet pans with buttered parchment paper.

2. In a mixer with a paddle attachment, combine the almond paste, sugar, and butter; beat until creamy. Add the eggs and beat until blended.

3. On low speed, add the cake flour and mix to combine.

4. Scrape the batter into the prepared pans and bake until set, about 25 to 30 minutes. Cool the cakes in the pans.

ASSEMBLY

1. Have ready two 7 x 3 1/2 x 2 1/2" (17.8 x 8.9 x 6.4 cm) terrine molds or loaf pans.

2. Measure and cut the almond cake to line the inside of the terrine molds. Fill the lined molds with the sour cream ice cream. Top each mold with a strip of almond cake. Freeze overnight.

RASPBERRY SAUCE	24 oz	680 g	fresh raspberries
	8 oz	227 g	granulated sugar
	4 liq oz	118 ml	water
	2 Tbs	30 ml	lemon juice

1. In a medium saucepan, combine the raspberries, sugar, and water. Bring to a boil; reduce the heat and simmer for 10 to 15 minutes, or until thickened.

2. Strain through a chinois to extract the seeds. Stir in the lemon juice. Chill.

VANILLA SABAYON SAUCE	4 oz	113 g	egg yolks
	4 oz	113 g	granulated sugar
	1	1	vanilla bean, split and scraped
	8 liq oz	237 ml	heavy cream
	8 oz	227 g	crème fraîche

1. Combine the yolks, sugar, and vanilla bean in a double boiler and whisk until pale and thick, about 4 to 6 minutes. Remove from the heat. Cool.

2. In a mixer fitted with a whisk attachment, whip together the cream and crème fraîche until soft peaks form. Fold into the yolk mixture. Strain through a chinois, discarding the vanilla bean. Place the sauce in a squeeze bottle and chill.

SPUN SUGAR CYLINDERS

14 oz	397 g	granulated sugar
8 liq oz	237 ml	water
2 oz	57 g	glucose

1. Place the sugar and water in a heavy saucepan. Cook over low heat, stirring constantly, until the sugar is dissolved. Add the glucose, stirring until it is combined with the syrup.

2. Increase the heat and bring the syrup to a boil, washing down the sides of the pan with a brush dipped in water occasionally. Bring the syrup to 310°F (154°C). Immediately remove the pan from the heat and plunge the bottom of the pan in cold water to stop the cooking process. Remove the pan from the water and allow the syrup to stand for a few minutes to thicken slightly.

3. Arrange 2 dowels over the edge of a table. Dip a cut-off whisk in the sugar and flick it back and forth over the dowels in a rapid motion to create the spun sugar. When enough of the sugar has formed, immediately wrap it around a 1" (2.5 cm) PVC tube to form a spun-sugar cylinder (see photo to the left). Repeat to form a total of 10 cylinders.

FINAL ASSEMBLY

26 oz/737 g fresh raspberries
Honey
Mint leaves
Pulled-sugar sticks

1. Pool the raspberry sauce on a dessert plate. Squeeze out a few dots of the sabayon sauce onto the plate.

2. Spread a thin layer of crème fraîche filling on the tart shell. Cover the filling with raspberries and drizzle with honey.

3. Place a 1" (2.5 cm) thick slice of sour cream terrine on one side of the plate. Top with a spun-sugar cylinder. Fill the cylinder with raspberries.

4. Unmold a warm pudding onto the other side of the plate. Place a raspberry tart on top of the pudding and top with a small scoop of raspberry sorbet. Place a sprig of mint next to the sorbet.

5. Garnish the plate with pulled-sugar sticks, raspberries, and mint leaves.

RHUBARB AND STRAWBERRY STRUDEL

KRISTA KERN

Pastry Chef, *Three Fish, Westerly, Rhode Island.*

Although strudel is generally considered Austrian in origin, most food historians agree that the original recipe was developed in Hungary and refined by the Austrians. The name comes from the German word for "whirlwind." "There is a reason this dessert looks the way it does," says Krista Kern, who first served it at a restaurant called Bang in Greenwich, Connecticut. "It was Asian cuisine, and a lot of it was vertical. This was my play on a spring roll, using a strudel but standing it up, and the dried rhubarb giving the air of firecrackers." The classic combination of strawberry and rhubarb is given fresh life when combined with bruléed lemon-ricotta cheesecake, lemon sabayon, and lemon meringue discs. Fresh strawberries, rhubarb sorbet, and pink peppercorn berry broth finish the presentation. "The pink peppercorn broth adds heat and spice that really complements rhubarb and strawberry," says Krista Kern. "It also gives it body."

YIELD: 6 SERVINGS

Special Equipment:
9 1/2" (24 cm) loaf pan
Six 1 1/2" (3.8 cm) diameter x 4" (10.2 cm) high stainless-steel tubes

MONT BLANC

MICHAEL HU

Executive Pastry Chef, *Waldorf-Astoria Hotel, New York.*

Named for the snow-capped mountain located at the border between France and Italy, this classic, autumn dessert usually consists of chestnut purée, and is quite heavy. Michael Hu's lighter variation consists of a dome of chocolate sorbet atop a chocolate sable, with chestnut mousse and whipped cream piped at the base, and chocolate sauce splashed in between. A chocolate fence surrounds all. Candied chestnuts in caramel and a white chocolate spiral finish the plate.

YIELD: 10 SERVINGS

Special Equipment:
Ten acetate strips, 1 3/4 x 11 1/2" (4.4 x 29.2 cm)
Twenty bamboo skewers

CHESTNUT MOUSSE			
1.5 lb	.68 kg	*fresh unshelled chestnuts, about 48 to 52*
1/2 tsp	3.4 g	*salt*
6 liq oz	177 ml	*milk*
6 liq oz	177 ml	*light cream*
3 oz	85 g	*granulated sugar*
1 1/2	1 1/2	*vanilla beans, split and scraped*
9 liq oz	177 ml	*heavy cream*
1.5 Tbs	7.5 ml	*dark rum*

1. Preheat oven to 400° (204°). Line 3 half-sheet pans with silicone baking mats.

2. In a bowl, combine the almond flour, confectioners' sugar, and all-purpose flour. Sift together twice.

3. In a mixer fitted with a whisk attachment, beat the eggs on high speed until doubled in volume. Fold in the sifted dry ingredients in three additions.

4. In a mixer fitted with a whisk attachment, combine the egg whites, one-third of the granulated sugar, the dried egg whites, and cream of tartar. Beat to soft peaks. Slowly add the remaining granulated sugar and beat until firm peaks. Fold the meringue into the egg-flour mixture; then fold in the melted butter.

5. Divide the batter into 3 equal parts and spread evenly onto the 3 prepared pans. Bake for 10 to 12 minutes until set; cool completely.

SEMISWEET CHOCOLATE MOUSSE

11 liq oz	325 ml	milk
11 oz	312 g	semisweet chocolate, such as Valrhona Extra Noir, finely chopped
.35 oz	10 g	gelatin sheets, softened in cold water
5.5 oz	156 g	egg yolks
5.5 oz	156 g	granulated sugar
18 liq oz	532 ml	heavy cream, whipped to soft peaks

1. In a saucepan, bring the milk to a boil. Add the chocolate; lower the heat and stir until the chocolate is melted. Add the drained gelatin to the chocolate mixture and stir until the gelatin is melted and the mixture is smooth. Remove from the heat.

2. In a large double boiler, whisk together the egg yolks and granulated sugar. Place the bowl over a bain-marie. Whisk until the mixture is pale and thick. Add the chocolate mixture to the egg mixture and whisk until well-combined.

3. Place the mixture over an ice bath and stir with a rubber spatula until it begins to congeal. Remove from the ice bath and fold in one-third of the whipped cream. Fold in the remaining whipped cream in two additions.

CAFÉ-WHITE-CHOCOLATE MOUSSE

11 liq oz	325 ml	heavy cream
2 Tbs	30 ml	Kahlua liqueur
1 Tbs	15 ml	coffee extract
1 tsp	4 g	instant espresso powder
4 liq oz	118 ml	milk
4 oz	113 g	white chocolate, such as Valrhona Ivoire, finely chopped
.24 oz	6.7 g	gelatin sheets, softened in cold water
2.6 oz	74 g	egg yolks
2.5 oz	71 g	granulated sugar

1. In a mixer fitted with a whisk attachment, combine the cream, Kahlúa liqueur, and coffee extract. Whip to soft peaks. Refrigerate until needed.

2. In a saucepan, bring the milk and espresso powder to a boil. Add the chopped chocolate and, over low heat, stir until the chocolate is melted and the mixture is smooth. Add the drained gelatin and stir until the gelatin is dissolved in the mixture. Remove from the heat.

3. Combine the egg yolks and sugar in a large double boiler and whisk until pale and thick. Add in the melted chocolate mixture and whisk until smooth.

4. Place over an ice bath and stir with a rubber spatula until the mixture begins to congeal. Remove from the ice bath and fold in one-third of the whipped cream combination. Fold in the remaining whipped cream in two additions.

COFFEE AND KAHLÚA SYRUP			
16 liq oz	473 ml	simple syrup
6 liq oz	177 ml	coffee
1 Tbs	15 ml	Kahlúa liqueur

Combine all the ingredients.

GANACHE GLAZE			
7 liq oz	207 ml	heavy cream
9 oz	255 g	Valrhona Guanaja chocolate, finely chopped

1. Place the chopped chocolate in a heat-proof bowl.

2. In a saucepan, bring the cream to a boil over medium-high heat. Pour the boiling cream over the chocolate. Let sit for about 30 seconds; stir with a rubber spatula until the chocolate is completely melted and the ganache is very smooth.

OPERA CAKE ASSEMBLY

1. Place a layer of the joconde on the bottom of a sheet pan. Spread half of the semisweet chocolate mousse evenly over the joconde. Place a second layer of joconde on top of the mousse. Spread the café-white-chocolate mousse over this layer. Top this with the third layer of the joconde and spread the remaining semisweet chocolate mousse over this layer. Freeze the cake for at least 3 hours to firm up the mousse layers.

2. Remove the opera from the freezer and pour the ganache glaze over the top of the cake, spreading it evenly with a metal spatula. (You may not need all of the glaze.) Refrigerate and allow the ganache to set completely.

3. Cut the glazed opera into 2 x 3" (5.1 x 7.6 cm) wedges as needed.

CHOCOLATE TOWERS			
3 lbs	1.4 kg	bittersweet chocolate, melted and tempered

1. Ladle melted chocolate into a plastic pyramid mold to completely fill. Turn the mold upside down and let the excess chocolate drip back into the bowl containing the tempered chocolate. Repeat to make 20 chocolate-lined towers. (If a second coat of chocolate is desired, repeat the above process after the first coat has set.)

2. Allow the towers to set at room temperature for at least one hour before filling with caramel mousse.

CARAMEL MOUSSE			
21 liq oz	621 ml	heavy cream, divided
3.5 oz	85 g	granulated sugar
2.75 oz	78 g	glucose
.5 oz	14 g	unsalted butter, at room temperature
3.25 oz	92 g	egg yolks
2 liq oz	59 ml	simple syrup
.41 oz	11.7 g	gelatin sheets, softened in cold water
		Cocoa Barry "prima" coating

1. In a saucepan, scald 6 liq oz (177 ml) of the heavy cream. Keep warm.

2. Whip the remaining 15 liq oz (444 ml) of heavy cream to soft peaks and refrigerate until needed.

3. In another saucepan, cook the granulated sugar and the glucose to a medium caramel color. Remove from the heat and stir in the butter.

4. Return the pan to low heat and slowly add the heavy cream. (The mixture will bubble up.) Stir until the mixture is well-blended and any hardened caramel has melted. Remove the caramel from the heat and set aside.

5. Combine the egg yolks with the simple syrup in a large heat-proof bowl. Place over a bain-marie and whisk until the mixture is thick and pale. Add in the drained gelatin and stir until the gelatin is dissolved and the mixture is smooth. Remove the bowl from the heat and stir in the caramel. Cool over an ice bath.

6. When the mixture starts to congeal, fold in the heavy cream in three stages.

7. Fill a pastry bag fitted with a plain tip with the caramel mousse and pipe the mousse into the chocolate towers. Chill until the mousse is set, about 2 to 3 hours.

8. Remove the filled chocolate towers from the plastic molds. With a heated knife, make 5 slits in each tower. These will eventually hold 5 marbled chocolate triangles. Fill a Wagner airless paint sprayer with Cocoa Barry "prima" and spray a fine mist evenly over the towers.

| MARBLED-CHOCOLATE | 12 oz | 340 g | dark chocolate, tempered |
| TRIANGLES | 2 lbs | 907 g | white chocolate, tempered |

1. On a work surface, randomly drizzle some of the melted dark chocolate. Before it sets and using an offset spatula, spread a thin layer of the white chocolate over the drizzled dark chocolate. This will create a marbled effect. Allow to set.

2. Cut out 140 triangles (7 per tower) of various sizes (see photo, page 82). There should be 20 of each size. Make sure that one of the sizes is such that the triangle will be at least as large as the top surface of the opera wedge. Make sure that one of the sizes is such that the triangle will cover the open end of the chocolate tower; this triangle should have a 1/2" (1.3 cm) hole cut from its center.

ASSEMBLY AND PLATING

20 pulled-sugar spirals
Chocolate sauce
40 fresh raspberries

1. Remove a caramel mousse-filled tower from the refrigerator. Have ready 7 marbled triangles of assorted sizes including one with a cut-out hole. Cut a 2 x 3" (5 x 7.6 cm) wedge from the refrigerated opera cake.

2. Insert a pulled-sugar spiral through the triangle with the hole. Insert 5 assorted triangles into the slits of the prepared tower.

3. On a dessert plate, place the wedge of opera cake slightly off-center. Arrange the assembled tower next to the cake, so that the cake will help support the tower. Top the cake with the triangle of similar size; it should not completely cover the glaze. Top the open end of the tower with the triangle that has the attached sugar spiral; it should completely cover the mousse.

4. Garnish the plate with dots and lines of chocolate sauce and 2 raspberries.

PETITS POTS DE CRÈME D'AUJOURD'HUI

PASCAL JANVIER

Pastry Chef, Instructor, Technical Manager, *Callebaut Barry Training Center, Pennsauken, New Jersey.*

Today's pot de crème "is a reworked version of an old French dessert that I have tried to modernize to suit the expectations of today's customers," says Pascal Janvier. The rich pot de crème recipe is intact, but the top is sprayed with white chocolate and it is further crowned with a chocolate tablet, with chocolate lines arranged in such a way that "I am playing with round, rectangular, and triangular forms," says Janvier. "With this plate you also have a square."

YIELD: 13 SERVINGS

Special Equipment:
Thirteen ramekins, 3 1/2" (8.9 cm) diameter and 1 1/4" (3.2 cm) deep
Wagner airless paint sprayer

POTS DE CRÈME			
	34 liq oz	1 lt	heavy cream
	8.5 oz	240 g	Chocolat-Amer 60% (extra-bitter chocolate)
	5.6 oz	160 g	Grand Caraque (unsweetened chocolate)
	8.5 oz	240 g	large egg yolks
	7 oz	198 g	granulated sugar
	4 drops	4 drops	red food coloring

1. Preheat a convection oven to 210°F (100°C). In a saucepan, bring the cream to a boil. Remove from heat; add the extra bitter and unsweetened chocolates to the hot cream and whisk until the chocolate is melted.

2. In a bowl, whisk the egg yolks and sugar together. Add some of the chocolate mixture to the yolk mixture to temper; add the remaining chocolate mixture. Add the food coloring.

3. Strain the mixture and pour it into the ramekins, filling them. Bake 20 minutes or until barely set (no water bath is needed). Refrigerate.

CHOCOLATE LINES	9 oz	255 g	dark couverture chocolate, tempered

1. Spread some of the chocolate onto acetate. Scrape with a wide-tooth comb to make 39 lines about 1/4" (.6 cm) thick and 6 1/2" (162.7 cm) long.

2. Let set and remove the strips from the acetate.

CHOCOLATE TABLETS	Extra Bitter Guayaquil 64%, tempered		

Spread some chocolate onto acetate. When it just starts to set, cut it into thirteen 1 x 1 1/2" (2.5 x 3.7 cm) tablets. Let it set completely and remove from the acetate. (You can also use tablet molds available from Cocoa Barry.)

ASSEMBLY	4 oz	113 g	white chocolate
	4 oz	113 g	cocoa butter
			gold leaf

1. Cover the rims of the ramekins. Melt the white chocolate and cocoa butter together and place in the airless paint sprayer. Carefully spray the pots de crème with the mixture.

2. Place a dot of gold leaf onto the center of each tablet.

3. Place 3 of the chocolate strips into a triangle shape on top of each ramekin. Place a chocolate tablet in the center of each.

CHOCOLATE CROISSANT BREAD PUDDING WITH SPECKY VANILLA ICE CREAM AND CARAMEL

MARSHALL ROSENTHAL

Executive Pastry Chef, *Trump Taj Mahal Hotel and Casino, Atlantic City, New Jersey.*

Bread pudding—an American classic recipe—is updated with croissants rather than brioche. "You have tart and sweet, warm and cold, smooth and crunchy on this plate," remarks Marshall Rosenthal. The classic chocolate and banana combination (via the caramelized bananas) is supported with caramel sauce, raspberry coulis, and vanilla-bean ice cream, for an all-American interplay of neutral, tart, and sweet flavors.

YIELD: 50 SERVINGS

BREAD PUDDING			
	2 lbs, 8 oz	1.13 k	day-old croissants, cut into 1/4" pieces
	24.5 oz	695 g	whole eggs
	5.2 oz	147 g	egg yolks
	1 lb, 4 oz	567 g	granulated sugar
	7.5 oz	213 g	extra-brute cocoa powder, sifted
	2 qts, 8 liq oz	2.13 lt	heavy cream (40%), divided
	2 liq oz	59 ml	bourbon vanilla extract

1. In a 20 qt (18.9 lt) mixer using a whisk attachment, beat the eggs, yolks, sugar, and 1 qt (.9 lt) of the heavy cream at low speed until blended. Gradually add the cocoa powder, vanilla, and the remaining heavy cream; mix until blended.

2. Strain the mixture into a large bowl. Add the croissant pieces, tossing them into the custard until they are well coated. Cover the custard and refrigerate for at least 4 hours.

3. Preheat the oven to 330°F (165°C). Lightly coat 4 oz (118 ml) ramekins with clarified butter. Spoon the custard into the ramekins. Place the ramekins in a hotel pan. Fill the pan halfway with cool water and bake 40 to 45 minutes, until set.

1. Invert a warm croissant pudding onto a dessert plate. Push the tip of the squeeze bottle containing the caramel filling into the center of the pudding. Squeeze out about 2 oz (57 g) of the filling into the center of the pudding, so that it spills out onto the plate. Make a cut halfway through the pudding and separate the two wedges slightly. Push the pointed end of one of the chocolate cones into the pudding. Place 2 raspberries into the cone. Dust the dessert with the confectioners' sugar. Place a choux garnish behind the pudding.

2. Garnish the plate with a few caramelized banana slices, a scoop of the specky vanilla ice cream, and the raspberry sauce.

LACE WAVE

PHILIPPE LAURIER

Executive Pastry Chef,
*Patisfrance USA, East Rutherford,
New Jersey.*

The classic miroir (or mirror cake) is given a Modernist makeover—apple-cinnamon mousse with layers of biscuit and succès is "glazed," though food colorings and Calvados are added to this glaze. White chocolate, milk chocolate, and dark chocolate comprise the lace. A chocolate cigarette covered in cinnamon powder, ("We could have used cinnamon sticks," says Chef Laurier, "but you can't eat it."), star-fruit, mini-apples (imported from China), and green-apple coulis finish the presentation.

YIELD: 12   SERVINGS

Special Equipment:
Twelve 3" (7.6 cm) oval ring molds, 1 3/4" (4.4 cm) high, about 6 oz (177 ml) capacity
Silicone baking mat

ALMOND MERINGUE	3 oz	85 g	almond flour
	2.5 oz	71 g	confectioners' sugar
	4 oz	113 g	egg whites
	1 oz	28 g	granulated sugar

1. Preheat oven to 300°F (149°C). Line a half-sheet pan with parchment paper.

2. In a bowl, whisk together the almond flour and confectioners' sugar until thoroughly blended.

3. In a mixer fitted with the whisk attachment, whip the egg whites and granulated sugar to firm peaks. Fold in the almond mixture.

94

4. Fill a pastry bag fitted with a plain tip (Ateco #4) with the almond meringue. Pipe 3" (7.6 cm) ovals onto the prepared pan. Bake for 25 to 30 minutes, until lightly browned. Let cool completely. Trim the meringues with a serrated knife to uniform size.

HAZELNUT-ALMOND BISCUIT			
3 oz	85 g	hazelnut flour
2 oz	57 g	almond flour
1 oz	28 g	all-purpose flour
3.25 oz	92 g	egg yolks
1.75 oz	50 g	whole eggs
10 oz	283 g	granulated sugar, divided
5.25 oz	149 g	egg whites

1. Preheat oven to 400°F (204°C). Line a half-sheet pan with parchment. Lightly butter the pan.

2. In a bowl, whisk together the hazelnut flour, almond flour, and all-purpose flour until well combined.

3. In a mixer fitted with the paddle attachment, beat the egg yolks, whole eggs, and 9 oz (255 g) of the sugar to a pale ribbon, about 5 to 6 minutes. On low speed, slowly add the dry ingredients until just combined. Do not overmix.

4. In a mixer with a whisk attachment, whip the egg whites with the remaining 1 oz (28 g) of sugar to firm peaks. Fold the meringue into the egg-flour mixture.

5. Spread the batter onto the prepared pan. Bake for 10 to 12 minutes. Allow to cool, then cut the cake into twelve 3" (7.6 cm) ovals.

CINNAMON-BAVARIAN CREAM			
8 liq oz	237 ml	milk
3 oz	85 g	granulated sugar, divided
.5 tsp	2 g	ground cinnamon
1.95 oz	55 g	egg yolks
.41 oz	11.7 g	gelatin sheets, softened in cold water
14 liq oz	414 ml	heavy cream, whipped to soft peaks

1. In a saucepan, bring the milk, 2 oz (57 g) of the sugar, and the cinnamon to a boil.

2. Whisk the yolks with the remaining 1 oz (28 g) of sugar until combined.

3. Temper the yolk mixture with the hot milk. Return to the heat and cook the mixture until it reaches the custard stage. Remove from the heat and stir in the drained gelatin. Pass the custard through a chinois. Cool over an ice bath. Fold in the whipped cream before the custard sets.

GREEN-APPLE SAUCE			
1.2 oz	34 g	egg yolk
3 liq oz	89 ml	simple syrup
14 oz	397 g	frozen green-apple purée, thawed
2 oz	57 g	granulated sugar
1/2	1/2	vanilla bean
.5 tsp	2 g	ground cinnamon
1	1	whole clove

3 oz	85 g	unsalted butter
2 liq oz	59 ml	lemon juice
1.5 oz	44 ml	Calvados
.41 oz	11.7 g	gelatin sheets, softened in cold water

1. In a double boiler, cook the egg yolks with the simple syrup to 165°F (74°C); set aside.

2. In a saucepan, combine the green-apple purée, granulated sugar, vanilla bean, cinnamon, clove, and butter. Bring to a boil, stirring constantly. Remove from the heat and stir in the lemon juice and Calvados. Whisk in the drained gelatin. Before the mixture cools add the yolk-syrup mixture.*

*Note. If this sauce is chilled, it will become very stiff and will have to be warmed gently before using.

CALVADOS-MIRROR GLAZE

15 oz	425 g	mirror glaze (from Patisfrance)
1.5 liq oz	44 ml	Calvados

Melt the mirror glaze in a saucepan. Remove from the heat and stir in the Calvados.

DRIZZLED-CHOCOLATE DECORATION

12 oz	340 g	dark chocolate, tempered
12 oz	340 g	milk chocolate, tempered
12 oz	340 g	white chocolate, tempered

ASSEMBLY

1. Arrange twelve oval ring molds on a parchment-lined sheet pan. Place one almond meringue in the bottom of each mold.

2. Fill a pastry bag fitted with a medium plain tip with the cinnamon Bavarian cream. Pipe a 1/2" (1.3 cm) layer of Bavarian cream onto each disc. Top with an oval of hazelnut-almond biscuit and gently press down. Pipe another 1/2" (1.3 cm) layer of Bavarian cream, leaving room for the Calvados-mirror glaze. Smooth over with the bottom of a small spoon. Chill until firm, about 2 hours.

3. If necessary, reheat the Calvados-mirror glaze to a pouring consistency. Cool slightly, so as not to melt the Bavarian cream.

4. Remove the desserts from the refrigerator. Spoon some of the mirror glaze over the Bavarian layer and swirl to create a thin even layer of glaze. Return to the refrigerator for 1 hour or until the glaze sets. (Do not glaze dessert more than one day ahead.)

6. Cut acetate into twelve 5" (125 cm)-long teardrop shapes. Cut additional acetate into 12 rectangular strips with an oval appendage so that it will partially wrap around the dessert (see photo, page 95).

7. Drizzle dark, milk, and white chocolates over the acetate cut-outs.

8. Allow the "rectangular" chocolate decorations to set slightly while unmolding the Bavarian desserts.

9. Wrap the drizzled-chocolate "rectangular" strips around the unmolded desserts and refrigerate until the chocolate is set, at least 15 minutes. Let the drizzled-chocolate ovals set completely at room temperature.

FINAL ASSEMBLY   *Whole mini-apples with stems attached**
Star fruit slices
Chocolate cigarettes dusted with ground cinnamon

    *Note. Mini-apples are available from Patisfrance, (800) PASTRY-1.

1. Remove a dessert from the refrigerator and remove the acetate. Place the ensemble on a dessert plate.

2. Sauce the plate with the green-apple sauce.

3. Remove the acetate from a teardrop decoration and place on the plate. Garnish the plate with two apple halves, a star fruit slice, and the chocolate cigarettes.

CHOCOLATE ANGEL FOOD CAKE

KRISTA KERN

Pastry Chef, *Three Fish, Westerly, Rhode Island.*

A cone of frozen white-chocolate parfait is topped with a Cointreau truffle; a ring of chocolate angel food cake shimmers under stars of sugar and a curl of chocolate tuile. Tangerine sorbet and citrus juices lend tang to this chocolaty plate. "When I first sketched this," reports Krista Kern, "it looked to me like something that hops on Mars. A planet hopper."

YIELD: 6 SERVINGS

Special Equipment: Six individual-size angel food cake pans

CHOCOLATE ANGEL FOOD	3.2 oz	91 g	all-purpose flour
CAKE	1.9 oz	54 g	cocoa powder
	10.5 oz	298 g	granulated sugar, divided
	10.5 oz	298 g	egg whites
	.25 tsp	2 g	salt
	1.5 tsp	5 g	cream of tartar
	1/4	1/4	vanilla bean, scraped
	1/8 tsp	.5 g	almond extract

1. Preheat oven to 350°F (175°C). Sift together three times: the flour, cocoa powder, and half of the sugar; set aside. In a mixer fitted with a whisk attachment, whip the egg whites, salt, and cream of tartar to soft peaks. Slowly add the remaining sugar and beat until stiff and shiny. Mix in the vanilla bean seeds and almond extract.

2. Fold the dry ingredients into the whites. Divide the batter evenly among six ungreased angel food pans. Bake for 20 minutes or until a cake tester inserted comes out dry. Hang the pans upside-down and cool for one hour. To unmold, run a knife around the sides of the pans and invert.

WHITE CHOCOLATE PARFAIT		
.1 oz	3 g	gelatin sheets
1.3 liq oz	38 ml	Cointreau
3.4 liq oz	101 ml	water
22 oz	624 ml	white chocolate, melted
2 oz	57 g	egg yolks
3.2 oz	91 g	egg whites
12 liq oz	355 g	heavy cream, whipped to soft peaks

1. Bloom the gelatin in cold water. In a saucepan, heat together the Cointreau and water. Wring the excess water out of the gelatin and melt it in the warm liqueur.

2. In a large bowl whisk the melted gelatin into the white chocolate. Whisk in the egg yolks and allow the mixture to cool.

3. In a mixer whip the egg whites to stiff peaks. Fold the whites into the white chocolate mixture. Gently fold in the whipped cream. If the mixture is very loose, refrigerate it until it has set just slightly.

4. Pipe the parfait into 2 1/2" (6.3 cm) parchment cones. Freeze overnight. Unwrap when ready to serve.

COCOA MERINGUES		
4.2 oz	119 g	egg whites
3.5 oz	99 g	granulated sugar
2 oz	57 g	confectioners' sugar
.4 oz	11 g	cocoa powder
2	2	tangerines, zest finely grated

1. Preheat oven to 275°F (135°C). In a mixer fitted with a whisk attachment, whip the egg whites to soft peaks. Mix in the granulated and confectioners' sugars. Add the cocoa powder and tangerine zest and whip until stiff and shiny.

2. Pipe the meringue into 3" (7.6 cm) diameter circles on parchment-lined sheet pans. Bake for 35 to 45 minutes or until crisp and dry.

TANGERINE SORBET		
32 liq oz	946 ml	water, divided
10.5 oz	298 g	granulated sugar
3 Tbs	82 g	corn syrup
16 liq oz	473 ml	tangerine juice, strained
1 tsp	1 tsp	lemon juice
to taste	to taste	Cointreau

1. In a saucepan combine 12 liq oz (355 ml) of the water, the sugar, and corn syrup and bring to a boil. Remove from heat and cool completely.

2. Combine the syrup with the tangerine juice and the remaining 20 liq oz (591 ml) of water. Add the lemon juice, adjusting according to taste, and the Cointreau. Refrigerate overnight.

3. Process the mixture in an ice cream machine, according to the manufacturer's instructions.

COINTREAU TRUFFLES

8 oz	227 g	Valrhona Manjari chocolate
1.5 oz	43 g	unsalted butter
4 liq oz	118 ml	heavy cream
2 oz	57 g	granulated sugar
3 liq oz	89 ml	Cointreau
2	2	tangerines, zest finely grated
12 oz	340 g	milk chocolate couverture

1. Melt together the Manjari chocolate and the butter over a double boiler. In a saucepan, heat the cream and sugar and add to the chocolate mixture. Stir until fully incorporated. Add the Cointreau, adjust according to taste, then the tangerine zest. Cover with plastic wrap and freeze until firm.

2. Remove the ganache from the freezer and form truffles with a melon baller. Return truffles to the freezer until firm.

3. Temper the milk chocolate. Either coat the truffles completely or drizzle them with chocolate. Refrigerate until set.

CHOCOLATE TUILES

3.5 oz	99 g	unsalted butter
5.9 oz	167 g	granulated sugar
4.7 oz	133 g	all-purpose flour
.8 oz	23 g	light cocoa powder
.5 tsp	2.5 g	cinnamon
3.8 oz	108 g	egg whites

1. Preheat a convection oven to 350°F (175°C). In a mixer fitted with a paddle attachment, cream the butter and sugar together until light. Sift together the flour, cocoa powder, and cinnamon; add to the butter mixture. Slowly mix in the egg whites.

2. On a silicone sheet pan lined with a baking mat, spread the batter through a stencil with lines 11" (28 cm) long and 1/2" (1.3 cm) wide. Bake for 5 to 6 minutes or until just barely firm. Remove from the oven and immediately wrap each tuile around a cone. Cool until set.

MILK CHOCOLATE SAUCE

1 pt	473 ml	heavy cream
2 oz	57 g	unsalted butter
1	1	cinnamon stick
21.3 oz	605 g	milk chocolate, chopped

1. In a saucepan bring the heavy cream and butter to a boil. Add the cinnamon stick. Remove from the heat, cover with plastic wrap, and let infuse for 15 minutes.

2. Remove the cinnamon stick and reheat the cream. Pour the hot cream over the chocolate and whisk until combined. Pour mixture into a squeeze bottle.

WHITE-CHOCOLATE CREAM

2.5 *liq oz*	74 ml	*heavy cream*
8 oz	227 g	*white chocolate, melted*
8 oz	227 g	*crème fraîche, at room temperature*

1. Heat the cream and add it to the white chocolate. Stir until combined. Stir in the crème fraîche.

2. Pour into a squeeze bottle with a wide tip. Refrigerate until ready to use.

CITRUS JUICE

56 oz	1.6 k	*honey mandarins*

1. Squeeze the juice from the tangerines and strain out the pulp. Hold in the refrigerator.

2. Let the juice come to room temperature before serving.

CARAMEL SHOOTING STARS

16 oz	454 g	*granulated sugar*
8 *liq oz*	237 ml	*water*
3 oz	85 g	*glucose*

1. Combine the sugar and water in a saucepan and bring to a boil, washing down the sides of the pan as necessary. Add the glucose and cook the sugar to a light caramel. Briefly immerse the bottom of the pan in cold water to stop the cooking process.

2. When the caramel has cooled and thickened just a bit, drizzle it off of a spoon onto parchment paper to create free-hand stars with a tail coming out of one point.

ASSEMBLY

Tempered chocolate discs, 3" (7.6 cm) diameter
Spun sugar
Tangerine segments

1. Place a cocoa meringue in the center of a 12" (30.5 cm) soup bowl and top with three 1 1/2 ounce (43 g) scoops of tangerine sorbet. Place a chocolate disc on the sorbet and top with an angel food cake.

2. Using a melon baller, scoop a small hole out of the fat end of each parfait cone. Place the cone, fat end up, in the center of the cake and stick a truffle in the hole of the cone.

3. Drizzle milk chocolate sauce around the top of the cake, being careful not to get sauce on the parfait.

4. In the center of the cake place a chocolate tuile, narrow end up, a spun-sugar spray, and two caramel shooting stars.

5. Pour citrus juice around the dessert. Squeeze a few white chocolate lines into the juice. Place 5 tangerine segments around the dessert, sprinkle the tuile with confectioners' sugar, and serve immediately.

CHAPTER **T**HREE

EQUIPMENT, MOLDS, AND MODERNISM

MICHAEL HU

Executive Pastry Chef
*Waldorf-Astoria Hotel,
New York.*

BORN: May 1967, Oahu,
Hawaii.
TRAINING/EXPERIENCE: Kapalua
Hotel Company; Michael's (self-
owned), Maui; Chart House
Restaurant Company; Zabar's,
New York; Ritz-Carlton, New
York; Grand Hyatt, New York.

*"In Hawaii as a boy, I spent a lot
of time running from island to
island because my family is so
large. To give you an idea, my
youngest brother got married recent-
ly. He couldn't have a big wedding—he could only invite our
family, which meant there were over
two thousand people there. We roasted ten pigs, tapped fifteen kegs of
beer. I come from a family that is
very used to putting on big parties,
so it is only appropriate that I work
for the Waldorf."*

KIM O'FLAHERTY

Pastry Cook
Essex House Hotel, New York.

BORN: February 1967,
Lowell, Massachusetts.
TRAINING/EXPERIENCE:
Newbury College, Boston;
Sweet Creations, Wakefield,
Massachusetts; White Barn Inn,
Kennebunkport, Maine; Ritz-
Carlton, San Francisco; Ritz-
Carlton, Boston.

*"The best advice I ever got? Take
your time. That means two things
to me. First, to create pastry, it
should be built and layered. Too
many chefs try to just throw it
together all at once. It should be
done in stages over a period of
weeks. If you just stop at the initial
stage, it might be fine, but if you
continue to work on it, you will
build a better product. And take
your time with your career. Many
American chefs try to jump into a
chef position without getting the
proper training. I'm taking the
slow route, so that by the time I'm
ready, I'll be a great chef. I got a
pastry chef position early, in 1991.
I didn't know what I was doing.
The customers were happy, but I
was not."*

Pastry chefs are familiar with this scene: you go into the office of the executive chef or food and beverage manager and request the purchase of a mold—or a comb or a lamp or a set of stencils. The questions start coming at you. The room grows warmer, as the line cooks pass by and glare at you.

"We in the pastry shop are always being blamed that we want so many little tools and molds," says Bo Friberg of The Culinary Institute of America at Greystone in St. Helena, California. "They say, 'John back there has his pot and his spoon and his skillet, what do you need all that stuff for?' But it's just the nature of the business. We do so many more specialized things than the hot kitchen. If you're using it to create an incredible dessert that is showy and sells, why not?"

Some pastry chefs solve this problem by purchasing the molds they want themselves. "I find it easier to just buy it myself," says Richard Leach of the Park Avenue Cafe. "If people are going to pick at me, I'd rather argue about ingredients." John Degnan of the Lodge at Koele, Lana'i Hawaii, has a budget to purchase equipment. "But I spend a lot of my own money on molds and equipment," he says, citing chocolate molds, small equipment for sugar, lamps, stencils, silpat mats, and silkscreens. "Quite often I pur-chase molds that the savory cooks can use," he adds. "The hot kitchen can use some of the plastic molds for garde-manger and the pantry area."

It is probably no coincidence that the burst of creativity in American pastry kitchens is occuring in the wake of remarkable improvements in equipment. The Modernist pastry chef, seeking unfamiliar shapes and abstraction, now has a wealth of it, and can produce in bulk. "What the equipment enables you to do is do in high volume what you used to do by hand," says Degnan. "It's an explosion in new materials and molds," enthuses Bo Friberg. "It's making things so much easier to make desserts looks showy." Every menu needs at least one "wow" dessert, says Friberg, because the restaurant down the street probably does.

The revolution in plated desserts might not have been pos-sible without the Demarle Company in France. These are the people who manufacture Silpat and Flexipans, two pieces of equipment that have changed the way chefs approach their work.

Silpat was actually created in the early 1980s, but has only been in wide use in the United States for the last few years. Silpat is made from a woven glass fabric covered with F.D.A.-approved, conformed food-graded silicone. It can be used in either the oven, the freezer, or the microwave, and is designed to replace paper or fat in a tray or pan. Excellent for use for chocolate work, sugar- and pastry-making. Silpat is responsible for many of the sinuous, gracefully curved, and exquisitely conformed shapes found in this volume. It also led the way for the second major advance: Flexipans.

Flexipans are made of some of the same materials as Silpat—silicone-coated, spun fiberglass with a knitted fabric underneath—and have comparable tolerances to temperature. Flexipans are sold as full-size cake pans or in single-serving, multicavity sheets, with anywhere from 15 to 30 cavities in each. Forms available include savarin, brioche, mini-cheesecake, muffin, madeleine, timbale, florentine, quichettes, pyramid, muffin, demi-sphere, petit four, cylinder, pomponette, oval, tartlet, Christmas log, heart, dariole, and others. These molds are guaranteed for 2,000 uses, but will probably last longer. They release frozen items and most baked goods extremely well, and clean-up is effortless.

Silicone baking mats are now being manufactured by several companies. Also relatively new in the pastry kitchen are Teflon-coated sheet pan liners; plastic production molds, for assembly; Zig templates, an alternative to the improvised cardboard and fish-tub plastic templates most chefs use. These new products join the armamentarium of molds long available to the pastry chef: tinned-steel molds in all of the forms mentioned above; metal rings, pyramids, demi-spheres, and tartlets; acrylic rings for cold preparations; plastic chocolate molds; wooden graining tools for chocolate work; cake-top stencils; aluminum angel food cake pans and bundt pans.

From this array of equipment, chefs are combining and improvising to create new looks for their desserts. "These molds give you flexibility to create new creations," agrees Philippe Laurier. "For example, you can do a crème brûlée in a Flexipan and put it in the freezer. Then you can use it as a disc inside another dessert, a mousse for example. How could you take it out of any other kind of mold?" Laurier has also cut yule logs and triangular forms into wedges, for fresh components on his plates.

STANTON HO

Executive Pastry Chef
Las Vegas Hilton Hotel.

BORN: April 1952, Honolulu, Hawaii.
TRAINING/EXPERIENCE: Kapiolani Community College (University of Hawaii), culinary program; Ecole Lenôtre, Paris; various hotels and resorts, Hawaii.

"Chefs must make a number of mistakes, major mistakes, as part of the learning process. I have personally learned a lot from mistakes, and that makes you a better person as far as swallowing your pride, admitting your mistake, and correcting it so that in the future it will be easy sailing, production-wise. This is the best way to improve yourself as far as timing, servicing, mise en place, ensuring that you have a lot of backups in your refrigerators—it's a constant awareness of what's around you."

RICHARD LEACH

Pastry Chef
Park Avenue Cafe, New York.

BORN: November 1965, Greenlawn, New York.
TRAINING/EXPERIENCE: The Culinary Institute of America; River Café, Aureole, L'Espinasse, One Fifth Avenue, Symphony Café, La Côte Basque, all in New York.

"I've been lucky. People have given me a chance to do what I want. Charlie Palmer first gave me a chance to try pastry. We started with small, simple stuff, but once we started building vertically, and we saw how people reacted to it, we went nuts for a few years. Some things are vertical, and some aren't. It's not a goal to make things that poke you in the nose. But a lot of the things I did in the beginning I don't do anymore; I found them to be a little heavy and not as refreshing. Now I'm going more toward lighter fruit items when possible. People need lighter food."

This restless search for new forms and new materials also creates new challenges for the chef. "A lot of people don't know the science of conduction of heat," says Judy Prince of J.B. Prince in New York. They need to know the materials (stainless steel is not a great conductor of heat, for example), how the contour and size of a mold will affect the way the ingredients will bake, how the fat content of a recipe will affect its release, and how that changes with the mold material.

Chefs also fashion their own equipment from materials found in hardware stores, plumbing stores, and plastic concerns, presenting yet another challenge to this equipment-intensive industry—many chefs don't know the properties of items they use. PVC piping, so popular among pastry chefs, can leach toxins into foods if not properly wrapped. "You don't want to fool around too much because metals react," says Krista Kern. "You need to know the properties of these metals. I've seen kitchens that use curtain rods. You just can't be sure of the metals the curtain-rod people used."

But the informed chef, master of his materials, is ready to take on the world. Michael Hu's Gianduja Mousse is contained in a unique triangle form—unique in that Hu, executive pastry chef at the Waldorf-Astoria, had a carpenter at his hotel make an original for him to his specifications, and then he made an acetate mold from that. "I was looking for this triangle, not a pyramid," recalls Hu. "You'd think this form could be found on a trophy or on a light fixture somewhere, but it wasn't. So we had the carpenter make it." He uses it to great effect, positioning it at a gentle diagonal, and then making it the eye of raspberry powder undulations, creating an attractive arrangement with an unusual color timbre that calls attention to a classic flavor combination.

Hu's Pineapple Financier is made from a hexagonal mold, and when combined with exotic touches—bubble sugar, slashes of chocolate—the overall effect of a written Chinese character. The fact is, the forms of the chocolate were completely last-minute-plating, and that any exoticism the plate conveys is purely in the eye of the hungry diner.

Kim O'Flaherty takes a wedge out of a familiar ring and stands it on its side for her Midnight Macadamia Torte. The form is echoed by the white chocolate ring, and chocolate lines rise up from the back, as if they are frets, and the entirety is a delicious musical note. Note also how the simple converging lines of powder off to the side add drama, sweep and, contrast to this circle-themed plate.

Pascal Janvier makes his Chocolate Basket from a demi-sphere mold, creating a sphere within a sphere, a cold form and a warm one, with all the homey associations of a basket. Richard Leach juxtaposes the cold, severe Chocolate Box with a loose drizzle of chocolate sauce on the plate, and playful positioning of triangle cookies on a quenelle.

Boundless creativity? A paradise of limitless possibilities? John Degnan is already seeing a sameness, and yet another challenge to the contemporary chef. "The drawback is that a lot of people are doing the same style of pastry with this equipment," he says. "What is emerging is a similarity of look. The challenge is to do something new with it."

BITTERSWEET CHOCOLATE BOXES WITH CHOCOLATE ESPRESSO SORBET

RICHARD LEACH

Pastry Chef, *Park Avenue Cafe,*
New York.

Espresso mousse is enclosed with cubes of chocolate cake in a thin chocolate box, and the flavor is reinforced by the chocolate espresso sorbet atop a chocolate meringue. Dots of espresso sabayon, chocolate tuiles, and drizzles of chocolate sauce finish the presentation. "The smear of white chocolate on the box is just for decoration," says Richard Leach. "When I first did the box it was solid, but then I started fooling around, piping lines and so on. Now I take a brush and swipe it with white chocolate. It breaks it up a bit. It's not enough to affect the taste."

YIELD: 14 SERVINGS

Special Equipment:
Fourteen 2 x 2 x 3" (5.1 x 5.1 x 7.6 cm) plastic boxes (available at office supply stores)
Silicone baking mat
2" (5.1 cm) high x 8 1/4" (21 cm) long triangular stencil

CHOCOLATE BOXES			
	12 oz	*340 g*	*white chocolate, tempered*
	28 oz	*794 g*	*bittersweet chocolate, tempered*

1. Using a small paintbrush, streak some of the tempered white chocolate on the inside of the boxes. Chill until set, about 15 minutes. Coat the inside of the boxes with tempered bittersweet chocolate. The layer of chocolate should be 1/16 to 1/8" (.16 to .32 cm) thick.

2. Place the boxes on a sheet pan and allow to set.

> *"You have to work clean with chocolate, and be delicate," says Richard Leach. "Polish molds well, and work on a clean, hard surface. The chocolate should be thin and easy for the customer to access. That's the trick to that box."*

Dessert shown on page 104.

CHOCOLATE ESPRESSO
SORBET

16 oz	454 g	bittersweet chocolate, chopped
2 oz	57 g	espresso roast coffee beans, crushed
4 oz	113 g	granulated sugar
48 liq oz	1.4 lt	water
1 Tbs	15 ml	coffee extract

1. Place the chopped chocolate in a bowl.

2. In a saucepan, combine the crushed coffee beans, sugar, water, and coffee extract; cook until the sugar is dissolved and the syrup is boiling.

3. Pour the hot syrup over the chopped chocolate and stir until completely melted.

4. Strain the mixture through a fine chinois and chill.

5. Process in ice cream machine, following manufacturer's intructions.

ESPRESSO SABAYON SAUCE

3 oz	85 g	egg yolks
3 oz	85 g	granulated sugar
1.5 Tbs	18 g	ground espresso beans
6 liq oz	177 ml	heavy cream
6 oz	170 g	crème frâiche

1. Combine the yolks, sugar, and ground espresso beans in a double boiler and whisk until pale and thick, about 4 to 6 minutes. Remove from the heat. Cool.

2. In a mixer fitted with a whisk attachment, whip together the heavy cream and crème frâiche until soft peaks form. Fold into the yolk mixture. Strain through a chinois; chill.

CHOCOLATE SAUCE

12 oz	340 g	bittersweet chocolate, finely chopped
2.25 liq oz	67 ml	light corn syrup
4.5 liq oz	133 ml	heavy cream

1. Place the chopped chocolate in a bowl.

2. In a saucepan, bring the corn syrup and cream to a boil.

3. Pour the hot cream over the chocolate and stir until completely melted.

CHOCOLATE CAKE

9.25 oz	262 g	all-purpose flour
1 Tbs	12 g	baking powder
.5 tsp	2.5 g	salt
5.25 oz	149 g	unsalted butter, at room temperature
12.25 oz	347 g	granulated sugar
2.5 oz	71 g	alkalized cocoa powder
5.5 oz	156 g	eggs
8 liq oz	237 ml	warm water

1. Preheat the oven to 325°F (163°C). Butter an 8 x 3" (20.3 x 7.6 cm) round cake pan. Dust with flour.

2. Sift together the flour, baking powder, and salt.

3. In a mixer with a paddle attachment, beat the butter until creamy. Gradually beat in the sugar and continue to beat until smooth. Turn the mixer off and add the cocoa powder all at once. On low speed, mix until combined. Gradually add the eggs, then slowly add the sifted dry ingredients and mix until combined. Slowly add the warm water and mix until smooth. Scrape the batter into the prepared pan and bake 60 to 70 minutes, or until the center is set. Cool for ten minutes; remove from pan and cool completely.

4. Cut the cake into small dice.

CUBE MOUSSE

2.5 *liq* oz	74 ml	milk
2 oz	57 g	unsalted butter
4 oz	113 g	bittersweet chocolate
2 tsp	4 g	finely grated orange zest
4 tsp	20 ml	coffee extract
3.5 oz	99 g	egg yolks
8 oz	227 g	granulated sugar, divided
20 oz	567 g	crème fraîche
11 *liq* oz	325 ml	heavy cream
22 oz	624 g	diced chocolate cake

1. Combine the milk, butter, chocolate, orange zest, and coffee extract in a double boiler and cook until the chocolate is melted and the mixture is smooth. Remove mixture from the heat and let it cool.

2. In a mixer fitted with a whisk attachment, whip the yolks and 4 oz (113 g) of the granulated sugar until pale and fluffy. Whisk into the melted chocolate mixture.

3. In a mixer with the whisk attachment, combine the crème fraîche, heavy cream, and the remaining 4 oz (113 g) of granulated sugar. Whip until soft peaks form. Fold into yolk-chocolate mixture. Fold in the diced chocolate cake.

4. Fill the chocolate boxes with mousse, leveling off the top with a spatula. Freeze until the mousse is firm.

DARK COCOA TUILES

3.35 oz	95 g	all-purpose flour
4 oz	113 g	confectioners' sugar
.75 oz	21 g	dark cocoa powder
4 oz	113 g	unsalted butter, softened
3.25 oz	92 g	honey
2 oz	57 g	egg whites

1. Preheat the oven to 300°F (149°C). Line a half-sheet pan with a silicone mat. Have ready a dowel or pipe for bending the tuiles.

2. Sift together the flour, confectioners' sugar, and dark cocoa powder.

3. In a mixer fitted with a paddle attachment, beat the butter until smooth. Add the honey and beat until pale. At low speed, add the sifted dry ingredients. Gradually beat in the egg whites and mix until the batter is smooth.

GIANDUJA MOUSSE

MICHAEL HU

Executive Pastry Chef, *Waldorf-
Astoria Hotel, New York.*

*The European classic favorite of chocolate and hazelnut is contrasted with the
slightly acidic tang of passion fruit. Michael Hu is particularly satisfied
with the look of the plate: "Visually it is complete," he says. "Everything is
working in harmony. There are some smooth dramatic lines in the raspberry
powder, the piped sorbet is very flowing, and the sugar connects everything
together."*

YIELD: 28 SERVINGS

**CHOCOLATE-COATED
PYRAMID MOLDS**

32 oz   *907 g*   *dark chocolate, tempered*

1. Using a template, cut out a piece of acetate with an X-acto knife, along the heavy
lines (as shown in the diagram below). Lightly score the dotted lines with the X-acto;
this makes the folding process easier. Fold along the dotted lines to produce a pyramid
with three triangular surfaces. The fourth surface gets folded in for stability. Each triangular surface measures 3 x 3 x 2" (7.6 x 7.6 x 5.1 cm), where the 2" (5.1 cm) side is the
base. Repeat to make 28 pyramids molds.

2. Ladle tempered chocolate into a mold to fill it completely. Turn the mold upside-down
to allow the excess chocolate to drip back into the bowl of tempered chocolate. Place the
mold on its side on a parchment-lined sheet pan. Repeat to make 28 chocolate-coated
pyramids molds. Let them set at room temperature for 1 hour.

GIANDUJA MOUSSE	13 oz	369 g	Gianduja chocolate, finely chopped
	3 oz	85 g	unsalted butter, cut in chunks
	3 oz	85 g	egg yolks
	2 oz	57 g	granulated sugar, divided
	4.2 oz	119 g	egg whites
	16 liq oz	473 ml	heavy cream, whipped to soft peaks

1. Melt the chocolate with the butter in a double boiler. Remove from the heat and set aside.

2. In a mixer with the whisk attachment, beat the egg yolks with 1 oz (28 g) of sugar to the ribbon stage. Fold into the chocolate mixture.

3. In a mixer fitted with a whisk attachment, whip the egg whites with the remaining 1 oz (28 g) of sugar to firm peaks. Fold the meringue into the chocolate mixture. Fold in the whipped cream.

4. Scrape the mousse into a pastry bag fitted with a plain tip. Pipe the mixture into the chocolate-coated pyramid molds, filling them completely. Level the top of the pyramids with a small spatula and chill until set, at least 4 hours.

PASSION FRUIT SORBET	19 oz	539 g	granulated sugar, divided
	.3 oz	9 g	stabilizer*
	44 liq oz	1.3 lt	water
	8.5 oz	241 g	glucose powder
	2.2 lbs	1 kg	frozen passion fruit purée

*Note. Stabilizer is available from Patisfrance, (800) PASTRY-1.

1. In a bowl, combine 9.5 oz (269 g) of the sugar with the stabilizer.

2. In a large saucepan, bring the water to a boil. Gradually mix the sugar mixture into the boiling water. Stir in the remaining 9.5 oz (269 g) of the sugar and the glucose. Return to the boil and boil for 20 to 30 seconds or until the syrup is clear. Remove from the heat.

3. When the syrup has stopped boiling, stir in the frozen passion fruit purée.

4. Process the mixture in an ice cream machine according to the manufacturer's instructions.

5. If not using immediately, freeze in a covered container. Otherwise, soften the sorbet to a piping consistency. Fill a pastry bag, fitted with a St. Honore tip, with the softened sorbet and pipe 28 servings of sorbet onto a cold parchment-lined tray. Freeze.

| COMBED-CHOCOLATE | 3 lbs | 1.36 kg | white chocolate, tempered |
| TRIANGLES | 1.5 lbs | .68 kg | dark chocolate, tempered |

1. Using an offset spatula, evenly spread a layer of white chocolate, about 1/8" (.32 cm) thick, on a work surface. Let stand for about 3 to 5 minutes until the chocolate is just beginning to set.

2. Drag a pastry comb through the chocolate to create straight lines.

3. Spread a layer of the dark chocolate across the white chocolate, filling the spaces created by the comb. Let chocolate set completely.

4. With a hot knife, cut out 28 triangles (3 x 3 1/2 x 2 1/2" / 7.6 x 8.9 x 6.4 cm).

5. With a hot knife, cut out 28 triangles (1 1/2 x 2 1/2 x 3" / 3.8 x 6.4 x 7.6 cm).

ASSEMBLY   *Dehydrated raspberry powder**
28 pink-pulled-sugar curls

    Note. Dehydrated raspberry powder is available from Fresh 'n Wild, Box 2981, Vancouver, WA (800) 222-5578.

1. Chill a dessert plate. Have ready two combed-chocolate triangles, one of each size. Take out a mousse-filled pyramid from the refrigerator and remove the acetate. Take out the dessert plate from the refrigerator and, using a decorative stencil, dust the plate with dehydrated raspberry powder.

2. Use a propane torch to heat a flat, heat-proof, metallic surface. Touch one side of the large combed-chocolate triangle to the heated surface. Immediately attach the warm side of the triangle to the cold plate, applying pressure so that it rests slightly elevated from the surface of the plate. Similarly, touch one side of the mousse-filled pyramid to the heated surface. Gently attach the pyramid to the elevated triangle.

3. Place the small triangle on the plate. Remove a serving of passion fruit sorbet from the freezer and place it on the triangle. Garnish the dessert with a sugar decoration. Serve.

MIDNIGHT MACADAMIA TORTE

KIM O'FLAHERTY

Pastry Cook, *Essex House Hotel, New York.*

O'Flaherty won the "Best Individual Plated Dessert" in the 1997 Patisfrance U.S. Pastry Competition for this dessert, a milk chocolate mousse with chocolate-covered macadamias and a passion-fruit curd inside. A chocolate blackout disc forms the base. Given the theme "The Age of Aquarius," O'Flaherty reproduced the signs of the zodiac in silkscreen on white chocolate. "It didn't really take too much time to put the visual design together," O'Flaherty recalls. "I love passion fruit, macadamias, and blackout cake, so I just put my favorite ingredients together."

Y I E L D :   1 2   S E R V I N G S

Special Equipment:
Twelve 3" (7.6 cm) ring molds
Wagner airless spray gun
Ring-shaped silkscreen (for a 3" (7.6 cm) ring)
Rubber trowel and decorating comb

CHOCOLATE BLACKOUT CAKE

8 liq oz	237 ml	brewed coffee
4 oz	113 g	unsalted butter
14 oz	397 g	granulated sugar
7.5 oz	213 g	all-purpose flour
pinch	pinch	salt
1 tsp	5 g	baking powder
2 tsp	10 g	baking soda
1.6 oz	45 g	cocoa powder, sifted
5.25 oz	149 g	whole eggs
8 liq oz	237 ml	buttermilk

1. Preheat oven to 350°F. Lightly grease a half-sheet pan. In a saucepan, combine the coffee and butter; heat until the butter is completely melted. Remove mixture from the heat and set aside.

2. In a mixing bowl, combine the sugar, flour, salt, baking powder, soda, and cocoa powder.

3. In another bowl, whisk together the eggs and the buttermilk. Whisk in the coffee mixture. While slowly whisking the dry ingredients, slowly pour in the liquid mixture. Whisk until all are combined. Pour the batter into the prepared pan and bake until set, about 30 minutes. Cool and cut into 2 1/2" (6.3 cm) discs.

ASSEMBLY   *Gold leaf*
            Mango sauce

1. Place one of the desserts on its side on a decorated plate. Lean one of the silkscreen rings against the dessert. Stand one of the chocolate wave garnishes vertically behind the dessert, with the attached end toward the plate.

2. Place a few graduated dots of mango sauce inside the triangle. Repeat with the remaining desserts.

CHOCOLATE BASKET WITH PRECIOUS HARVEST

PASCAL JANVIER

Pastry Cook, Instructor, Technical Manager, *Cocoa Barry Training Center, Pennsauken, New Jersey.*

"To me, chocolate should be treated like gold," says Pascal Janvier. *Cocoa sorbet rolled in cocoa powder is served in a chocolate basket. "I tried to do it, simply but nicely, to give a picture of preciousness."*

YIELD: 15 SERVINGS

Special Equipment:
5.5" (14 cm) diameter plastic demisphere molds, available from ABC Emballuxe (514) 381-8845

CHOCOLATE SORBET

5.3 oz	*150 g*	*Cocoa Barry Extra Brute, cocoa powder*
17.6 oz	*499 g*	*granulated sugar, divided*
58 liq oz	*1.7 lt*	*mineral water*
4.4 oz	*125 g*	*inverted sugar*
0.4 oz	*10 g*	*sorbet stabilizer, such as Gel Glace from Patisfrance*

1. In a bowl combine the cocoa powder and 14.1 oz (400 g) of the sugar.

2. In a saucepan, heat the mineral water until simmering. Remove from the heat and add the cocoa mixture, then the inverted sugar. When mixture cools to 113°F (45°C), add the stabilizer and the remaining 3.5 oz (99 g) of sugar.

3. Process in an ice cream machine according to the manufacturer's instructions. Using a 5 to 6 ounce (141 to 170 g) scoop, form the sorbet into perfectly round balls and freeze.

CHOCOLATE LACE DISH

60 oz/1.7kg Chocolat-Amer (extra-bitter) chocolate, tempered

1. Put some of the chocolate in a cornet and pipe 15 to 20 lines going in all directions in the demi-sphere molds.

2. Put the rest of the chocolate in a pastry bag with a 1/8" (.3 cm) star tip and pipe another 15 to 20 lines. Scrape the excess chocolate off the tops of the molds. Refrigerate for 30 minutes or until set, then unmold.

The chocolate lace is piped in a demi-sphere mold. Using 2 different pipes, there is a texture to one of the lines. Baking chocolate with a low cocoa butter content is used, so that the tempered chocolate remains thick and holds the line.

ASSEMBLY   *Gold leaf*
            Extra Brute cocoa powder

1. Cover the rim of each basket with gold leaf. Holding the basket with the rim at a 45° angle, rub the bottom on a warm surface until it just begins to melt. Place the basket on a serving plate and hold until set.

2. Roll the frozen balls of sorbet in cocoa powder and place in the chocolate lace dishes.

RASPBERRY TOWER

STAN HO

Executive Pastry Chef, *Las Vegas Hilton Hotel.*

"All the desserts I make are on the light side," says Stanton Ho. *"It's very appealing after a heavy meal. I try for an eye-catching appearance—the drama of this tower, for example. It's like a sales and advertising gimmick when it passes by the tables."* Here, Italian meringue is folded into the raspberry mousse to give it a light consistency. The raspberry coulis on the bottom enhances the flavor of the fruits as well as the mousse, to create a well-balanced combination. A pulled-sugar floral arrangement completes the picture.

YIELD: 16 SERVINGS

Special Equipment:
Six clear, plastic, fluorescent light-protector tubes, 14" (35.6 cm) long x 1 1/4" (3.2 cm) diameter, available at electrical supply stores
Wagner airless spray gun

RASPBERRY MOUSSE

12.3 oz	350 g	raspberry purée
.25 oz	7 g	gelatin sheet, softened in cold water
1 Tbs	5 ml	lemon juice
9 liq oz	250 g	heavy cream, whipped to soft peaks
7 oz	198 g	Italian meringue

1. Place about half of the raspberry purée in a large bowl and heat over a water bath.

2. Drain the gelatin sheets and add to warm purée. Whisk the purée until the gelatin is dissolved. Remove from heat and whisk in remaining raspberry purée and lemon juice.

3. Cool over an ice bath.

4. Fold the whipped cream into the cooled raspberry mixture. Fold in the meringue. Refrigerate until set.

> *With the high volume Stanton Ho must produce every day for his hotel, the chef must be concerned with freshness and storage. "The Italian meringue stores very well cooked, so that there's less chance of bacterial growth," says Chef Ho. "A percentage of alcohol is a standard item in our recipes. When I have banquets for two thousand or three thousand, I have a tendency to put it in, for flavor and as a preservative."*

RASPBERRY COULIS	17.6 oz	500 g	*fresh raspberries*
	4.6 oz	130 g	*granulated sugar*

1. In a food processor with the steel blade, combine the raspberry purée and granulated sugar and process until blended.

2. Refrigerate until needed.

WHITE CHOCOLATE DISCS	9.7 oz	275 g	*white chocolate, tempered*

1. Spread the tempered white chocolate onto parchment paper evenly to make a 1/8" (.32 cm) thick layer. When slightly set, but still pliable, use a 1 1/2" (3.8 cm) round cutter to cut out 16 discs. Allow to set completely.

MARBELIZED CHOCOLATE	12 oz	340 g	*white chocolate, tempered*
TOWERS	3 oz	85 g	*semisweet chocolate, tempered*

1. Using a Wagner airless spray gun, spray some warm semisweet chocolate into both ends of one of the plastic tubes. Once the semisweet chocolate starts to set, quickly pour about 2 oz (57 g) of the warm tempered white chocolate into the tube. Roll the white chocolate around in the tube. The rolling motion achieves both a marbling effect and an even thickness. The chocolate layer should be 1/16" (.32 cm) to 1/8" (.16 cm) thick.

2. Repeat to make 6 marbleized tubes. Chill until set. The chocolate will disengage from the tubing when the chocolate sets. Slide the chocolate out of the tubes and cut into 4" (10 cm) pieces at an angle, using a hot wire cutter. Straighten the cuts by sliding the ends onto a hot flat griddle. At this point, attach a white chocolate disc to the base of each tower.

ASSEMBLY

Pulled-sugar flowers and flourishes
Fresh raspberries and assorted fruit

1. Spoon some raspberry coulis onto a dessert plate to create a triangle extending across the plate.

2. Fill a pastry bag fitted with a medium plain tip (Ateco #4), with raspberry mousse. Pipe the mousse into a chocolate tower. Insert a pulled-sugar flower and a few flourishes into the mousse and garnish the plate with raspberries and assorted fruit.

PINEAPPLE FINANCIER CAKE WITH POPPY SEED PARFAIT AND CHERRY SAUCE

MICHAEL HU

Executive Pastry Chef, *Waldorf-Astoria Hotel, New York.*

The flavors of the Mediterranean and the Tropics blend seamlessly in this refreshing finale. "Poppy seed parfait is definitely one of my favorites," says Michael Hu. "Pineapple goes well with almonds and hazelnuts, and the cherry sauce provides a nice contrast." A screen of bubble-sugar finishes the plate.

YIELD: 28 SERVINGS

Special Equipment:
Twenty-eight 4 oz (118 ml) hexagonal ring molds
Twenty-eight 2 oz pyramid molds
Silicone baking mat

POPPY SEED PARFAIT

5 oz	142 g	poppy seeds
4.6 oz	130 g	egg yolks
6 oz	170 g	granulated sugar
.75 oz	21 g	honey
2.5 liq oz	74 ml	Grand Marnier or other orange-flavored liqueur
2	2	vanilla beans, split and scraped
24 liq oz	710 ml	heavy cream, whipped to soft peaks

1. Spread the poppy seeds on a sheet pan and bake in a 350°F (177°C) oven for 15 to 20 minutes. Cool and reserve.

2. Combine the egg yolks, sugar, honey, Grand Marnier, and vanilla seeds in a double boiler and whisk until pale in color and thickened, about 10 minutes. Whisk until cool over an ice bath.

3. Fold in the whipped cream and poppy seeds. Pour into the pyramid molds and freeze.

ROASTED PINEAPPLE

7.5 lb	3.4 kg	peeled and cored fresh pineapple
12 oz	340 g	light brown sugar
6 oz	170 g	unsalted butter, melted

1. Preheat oven to 375°F (191°C). Cut the pineapple into 1" (2.5 cm) chunks.

2. Place the pineapple chunks, sugar, and butter in a large roasting pan and toss to coat.

3. Bake for 25 to 35 minutes or until the pineapple chunks are golden brown and lightly caramelized. Stir occasionally to keep the pineapple chunks from sticking. Let cool.

4. Reserve 84 chunks for the cake and dice the remaining ones for the compote.

PINEAPPLE FINANCIER CAKE

30 oz	850 g	unsalted butter
11 oz	312 g	almond flour
32 oz	907 g	confectioners' sugar
11 oz	312 g	all-purpose flour
27 oz	765 g	egg whites
2.25 liq oz	67 ml	dark rum

1. Preheat oven to 350°F (177°C). Line a sheet pan with a silicone mat. Butter the hexagonal molds and place them on the prepared pan.

2. In a saucepan, melt the butter and cool slightly.

3. In a large bowl, combine the almond flour, sugar, and all-purpose flour.

4. In a mixer fitted with a whisk attachment, whisk the egg whites until foamy. Add the flour mixture and mix until just combined. Gradually add the melted butter and mix until blended. Stir in the rum. Let the batter rest for 1 hour.

5. Place 3 chunks of roasted pineapple in each mold. Fill the molds three-quarters of the way with batter. Bake 25 to 30 minutes or until golden. Remove the cakes from the molds and cool.

CHERRY SAUCE	2.2 lb	1 kg	cherry purée
	4 oz	113 g	glucose
	2 liq oz	59 ml	lemon juice

1. In a large saucepan, combine the cherry purée and glucose and boil for one minute. Remove from the heat and stir in the lemon juice.

2. Strain and chill.

| SUGAR GARNISH | 4 oz | 113 g | isomalt |
| | as needed | as needed | powdered food coloring |

1. Preheat oven to 350°F (175°C). Line a half-sheet pan with a silicone baking mat, smooth-side-up. Sprinkle the mat with the isomalt. Sprinkle the isomalt with the powdered food coloring, as desired.

2. Place another baking mat, smooth-side-down, over the isomalt covered mat. Bake the isomalt about 7 minutes.

3. Allow the sugar to cool for 20 minutes. Peel off the top baking mat. Break the bubble-sugar into various shapes and set aside to garnish the desserts.

ASSEMBLY   *Tempered chocolate triangles*

1. Decorate a dessert plate with the cherry sauce.

2. Place a financier cake in the center of the plate. Top with about one tablespoon of the compote. Unmold a poppyseed parfait and place it over the compote.

3. Arrange a bubble-sugar garnish and 2 chocolate triangles on the parfait.

Making the bubble-sugar garnish.

CHAPTER **F**OUR

MODERNIZING
GARNISHES

JOHN DEGNAN

Executive Pastry Chef,
*The Lodge at Koele, Lana'i,
Hawaii.*

BORN: 1965, Rockaway Beach,
New York.
TRAINING/EXPERIENCE: New
York City Technical College;
Patisserie Lanciani, Pierre
Hotel, Rainbow Room, Ritz-
Carlton, Sea Grill, Omni
Berkshire Hotel, all in New
York.

*"I liked the technical side of produc-
ing pastry at first. I didn't have a
great background in food, so the
challenge for me was learning flavors and textures. It's an ongoing
education. I learn a lot from chefs,
and not just pastry chefs, who teach
me about flavors. On the artistic
side, I see the forms in my head and
I start to play with them. Then I
visualize flavors and the dessert
kind of hits me. Of course it doesn't
necessarily work right the first time.
You have to work it three and four
times, get the opinions of the other
chefs, push it forward until you get
it the way you want. Flavor and
presentation are both important.
Flavor is most important, but you
want a 'WOW' factor."*

ERIC PEREZ

Executive Pastry Chef,
*Ritz-Carlton Tyson's Corners,
Virginia.*

BORN: June 1964, Toulouse,
France.
TRAINING/EXPERIENCE:
apprenticeship, various pastry
shops, including La Coste in
Toulouse; French embassy, Ritz-
Carlton Pentagon City, both in
Washington, D.C.

*"It should taste as good as it looks—
that's pretty much the basic philoso-
phy of pastry. You should love eat-
ing pastry. You cannot be as involved
unless you love to eat food, period.
That is the way you develop your
palate and your taste. Of course, to
become a pastry chef involves a lot of
things not pastry—learning to deal
with people, psychology. I like that
part. You give people the passion—
what someone else gave to you, you
give to them."*

"So you're a pastry chef. Create a dessert for me. See if
you can't arrange it so that some components are
cold, others hot; some tangy, some sweet. I want smooth
textures, but also some crunch. Remember that it must be
made in huge numbers by a few people in a small kitchen;
that it must be carried intact by a frazzled waiter to a table
way upstairs; that it must be priced to earn a profit; and that
it must taste wonderful. Oh, and while you're at it, design
the plate in a pleasing yet provocative manner. Be mindful
of line, form, texture, and color. Remember that line is not
simply line. A jagged line can convey energy, a horizontal
line power, while a vertical line is strong and formal, and a
curved line is sensuous. Nor is color simply color; you must
sort out hue, intensity, and value. Remember that hot colors advance while cool ones recede. You want balance, but
not blandness. You want informal balance—an aesthetic
arrangment of dissimilar forms. You want to evidence variety, emphasis, unity, and spacial order."

Little wonder that many culinary schools, including The
Culinary Institute of America, offer a visual composition
course. The variety of garnishes available to complement
the variety of central forms is enough to test any kitchen
artist's mettle.

It is in garnishing that chefs go overboard or go blah, where
the plate is ghastly or ga-ga, and where the compositional
sense of the chef is tested. We will deal with sauce in its own
chapter, but garnishes in general—cookies, fruit, nuts,
frozen items, and chocolate in all their forms—are much
more important in composition desserts than in rustic
desserts or in traditional European slice-and-sauce plates.

So what are some guiding principles to proper garnishing,
even in an outlandish Modernist dessert?

"I have no rules about garnishing because garnishing is a
very personal feeling about finishing a plate," says Pascal
Janvier of Cocoa Barry. "You can give the same ingredients
to ten chefs and you would have ten different treasures. I try not to impose any rules, except
that ingredients should be fresh."

So there *are* rules to garnishing and the chefs can cite a few, but if the reader's incipient
Modernist sensibilities start to twitch at the mention of rules, wait. There will be enough
exceptions to each rule to create chaos and tail-chasing.

Keep it simple. "It should promote the dessert and should not overpower," says Jacquy
Pfeiffer. "You should not spend 75 percent of your time on the garnish. It should be the
other way around. Don't overgarnish. Don't put one garnish atop another. For example,
sprinkling something over a rosette—you kill the first with the second."

"Garnishes take a lot of time to make, or some do," says Jemal Edwards, "and if you're pressed
for time in the kitchen, you want something that is simple and beautiful and doesn't take a
lot of time to do. Something you can make twenty or thirty of at a time."

Everything on the plate should be edible. "Sugar is probably the easiest way to make a WOW dessert for a customer," admits Bo Friberg. "Unfortunately, it's edible but not edible. You can cut your gums on that." "It should be edible," agrees Richard Leach. "Not bulky or thick. Delicate enough so that people can eat it."

Sebastien Canonne of the French Pastry School in Chicago agrees, but can think of an example when a large, overblown, inedible garnish is called for: when the client requests it. "Customers expect a lot of show, and that's why in upscale hotels they ask the chef to come up with some sugar work. A big sugar cage, for example," says Canonne. "If that's what they want, they will be happy. We won't be so happy, but we do it. If it's not really necessary, you try to talk them out of it."

Thaddeus Dubois of the Duquesne Club in Pittsburgh can sympathize. "Pastry chefs are in the hospitality business. We are in the business of pleasing people," he says. "If someone comes in and wants a sugar or caramel thing two feet high, we're in the business of providing it."

Wayne Brachman of Mesa Grill in New York doesn't believe garnishes should just be edible. "They should *taste good*," he says. "Edible is a dime a dozen. Hay is edible."

A garnish should promote harmony in flavor. "I like to follow through," says Krista Kern. "Everything should relate to the primary or secondary flavor." Richard Leach of the Park Avenue Cafe believes that a garnish should "provide an accent flavor for the main component. I go for one component with some small back textures."

"The garnish can contrast the flavor, but it's usually a good idea to remind the diner of the flavor," says Sebastien Canonne. "Apple chips for an apple dessert, or caramel. It is a delicate thing. Try to remind the customer what's inside with the garnish. Sometimes you can play with garnish to contrast. If something is not really sweet, you might have a tuile or sugar to bring sweetness or vice versa."

A garnish should provide a contrast in texture to the main component. "It should provide crispness if the dessert is smooth," says Sebastien Canonne, "but you don't want to add what's not needed. This is one of the biggest mistakes that people without classic training make. If the garnish can add to the dessert without taking over the dessert or becoming the dessert, it's okay. It should be a little thing. If you don't know what you're doing, stay with sautéed fruit, or sauce." Madeleines, tuiles, financier, or macaroons pair well with sorbet or ice cream, he says. With cake, a good sauce. With a warm dessert, a compote.

A garnish should add height. "People put a lot of effort into sauce painting and marbleizing, which is fine, there is no rule that says you can't," explains Stanton Ho of the Las Vegas Hilton. "I would concentrate more of my efforts on height. That way it becomes a saleable marketing device. Sauces can't be seen as they're carried through the dining room."

SEBASTIEN CANONNE

Co-owner, *Ecole de Patisserie Francaise, Chicago.*

BORN: October 1968, Amiens, France.
TRAINING/EXPERIENCE: apprenticeship, École Hotelière, Normandy; apprenticeship, Gaston Lenôtre; La Côte St. Jacques, Burgundy; Beau Rivage Palace, Geneva; Hotel Palace Euler, Basel; St. Germain, Ritz-Carlton Hotel, Chicago.

"In this country, a chef must be both creative and a businessman, and this is very difficult. First, though, you have to love the job. You can't make something nice if you don't feel it. You have to be a craftsman, to like to work with your hands. You have to have a business sense, but you can't be too businesslike to be the best, because this is an art which is a little bit of a science."

DONALD WRESSELL

Executive Pastry Chef,
*Four Seasons Hotel,
Beverly Hills, California.*

BORN: 1960, Issaquah, Washington.
TRAINING/EXPERIENCE: apprenticeship with Mark Randolph; Washington Athletic Club, Sorrento Hotel, and Westin Hotel, all in Seattle; Watergate Hotel, Washington, D.C.; Breakers Hotel, Long Beach, California; Four Seasons Hotel, Philadelphia.

"I like what I do, and I like the life of the pastry chef. I have exposure to things I wouldn't if I were some other kind of craftsman. I wouldn't travel in Europe and the States, experience life the way I have, eat great meals, meet fantastic people. It's a lifestyle choice more than a job, because the job is never over. You're constantly educating yourself. Mark Randolph (owner of Pastries by Randolph in Virginia) instilled into me that whenever you make a plate or a cake and you think it's really great, you have to find something about it that you would do better next time. You can never say, 'That's great, that's as good as it's ever going to be.' Give it the credit it deserves, but scrutinize it."

RICHARD RUSKELL

Pastry Chef,
The Phoenician,
Phoenix, Arizona.

BORN: November 1956,
Nebraska.
TRAINING/EXPERIENCE: French
Culinary Institute, New York;
Le Royal Grey, France; Hotel
Maxim's, Stanhope Hotel, both
in New York.

"Today's pastry chef tends to want
to include everything on a tiny
plate. I've started to come away
from that, and simplify—going
back and back and back to the
basics. People who come to the shop,
students especially, will say to me,
'Oh I want to make showpieces, I
want to pull sugar, and this and
that. . . .' and I say, 'Yeah, don't
we all want to sit down and pull
sugar? I would rather have you
make a little éclair or tart that is so
perfect, so nice, that I want to eat
the whole thing.'"

Contrast, yes, but harmony too. Simplicity, yes, but showbiz pizzazz as well. Rules, you bet, but exceptions too. To the Modernist chef, there are no absolutes. Only personal taste and customer whims.

But a general statement about the aesthetic value of a composition dessert can be made based on the desserts presented here. It is this: If the main component, or prominent forms, of a dessert are executed with precision and professionalism, the eye will forgive—it will admire—some looser forms and compositions on the plate. If the cuts are straight on a cake or cookie, the sugar can be haywire; if the surfaces are smooth on a glazed piece, the sauces can be splattered at random; if the fruits are fresh and chosen for perfect form, then they can be arranged in an asymmetrical way. One other observation: it is common for chefs to include a sugar spiral or rod to subtly bind disparate forms together.

Examples? The perfection of Sebastien Canonne's Raspberry Vanilla Blossom and the chocolate leaf that crowns it allows the eye to enjoy, and accept, the odd puff of sugar, the jumbled arrangement of chips, fruit, a coil of sugar, a berry impaled on a silly fork. Likewise, the precision of Kim O'Flaherty's Almond Sourdough Cake, the craft of the cookie that crowns it, allows us to accept the anarchic saucing as artful.

In this chapter you see many familiar forms—demi-spheres and rings particularly—that are enhanced by the accompaniment of more dramatic, severe, risky forms. See how the clever, if ordinary, ring that makes up Eric Perez's Chocolate and Pear Mousse is completely upstaged by the magnificent, towering chocolate cone, the chocolate curl that hugs it, the chocolate sphere that crowns it. Or how Stanton Ho's Dome of White Chocolate Mousse is lent an exotic air by the "serpentine" cookie that coils around it. Likewise, the simple geometric form of Richard Ruskell's Chocolate Cone is given delirious motion by wheel cookies artfully placed at odd angles.

A brownie, a homespun dessert if ever there was one, is rendered mysterious and powerful through an ultra-modern treatment: Philippe Laurier has elected to dress it up with sinister tendrils of chocolate, a looming cookie, and a pool of sauce, giving the plate a wild, hypnotic appeal.

Sometimes form simply follows function: The "sail" cookie dominates John Degnan's Asian Rice Torte for the simple reason that the chef wanted to hide the iffy attractiveness of rice in a dessert.

The chefs offer startling Modernist imagery: Sebastien Canonne's Sweet Dream Parfait, with its cookie-as-a-warped-clock-hand and the cocoa dusting of clock numbers vanishing dramatically; Norman Love's Banana Mousse and its pure geometric forms—cones so severe they are vanishing into lines, a demi-sphere with chocolate glazed to perfection, a curl of chocolate dangling in air to lessen the severity; John Degnan's Passion Fruit Mousse, perched on a chalice-like pedestal, and partially rimmed by a soaring cookie, like an earthquake remnant.

"The first thing the customer will buy with is his eyes, but the second time he will buy with his mouth," says Bo Friberg of The Culinary Institute of America. "So if it looks great but doesn't taste good, he will not buy it again. It should be showy but also taste great. There is, sometimes, a compromise situation." Sometimes, but not here. These plates exhibit take-no-prisoners, pedal-to-the-metal brashness; full flavor, startling presentation, weary kitchen staff.

PASSION FRUIT MOUSSE ON A CARAMEL CONE

JOHN DEGNAN

Executive Pastry Chef, *The Lodge at Koele, Lana'i, Hawaii.*

Flavors from the same region generally blend well, as this dessert attests: Pâte à cigarette-decorated joconde encircles, and forms the base for, the light, airy, and refreshingly tart mousse. The sweetness of the mangoes blends well with the mousse, while the coconut sauce enhances both flavors and provides visual punch. "I served this at my wedding and at the James Beard House," says John Degnan. "It's always been a favorite."

YIELD: 16 SERVINGS

Special Equipment:
Sixteen ring molds, 2 1/2" (6.25 cm) diameter x 1 1/2" (3.75 cm) high
Wagner airless paint sprayer
5" (125 cm) metal cream horns

PÂTE À CIGARETTE	4 oz	113 g	unsalted butter, melted
	4 oz	113 g	confectioners' sugar
	3.25 oz	92 g	cake flour
	1 oz	28 g	cocoa powder
	4 oz	113 g	egg whites

1. In a mixer fitted with a paddle attachment, mix together the butter and sugar. Sift the flour and cocoa powder together and add half to the butter mixture. Mix until combined and scrape down the side of the bowl. Slowly add the egg whites and mix until fully incorporated. Add the remaining dry ingredients and mix just until combined.

2. Put the batter in a cornet. On a half-sheet silicone baking mat pipe rows of triangles across the shorter side, staying within 1" (2.5 cm) columns. Freeze until ready to use.

JOCONDE	6.4 oz	182 g	eggs
	4.5 oz	128 g	granulated sugar
	4.6 oz	130 g	almond flour
	3.9 oz	110 g	egg whites
	1.2 oz	34 g	unsalted butter, melted
	2 oz	57 g	cake flour

1. Preheat the oven to 375°F (190°C). In a mixer combine the eggs, sugar, and almond flour; whip until very thick and light in color. Whip the egg whites to soft peaks and fold into the flour mixture. Fold in the melted butter followed by the cake flour.

Dessert shown on page 132.

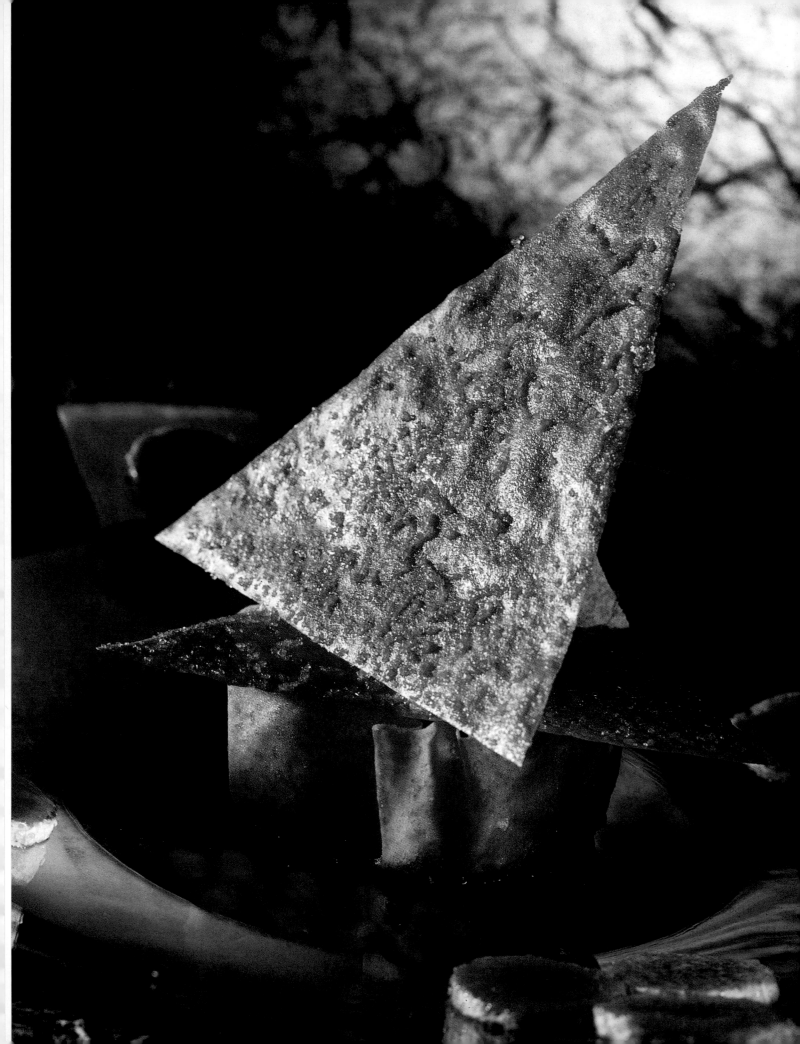

1. Preheat oven to 375°F (190°C). Combine all ingredients in a 9 x 13" (22.3 x 33 cm) baking pan and cover tightly with aluminum foil.

2. Bake, stirring occasionally, for 1 to 1 1/2 hours or until the rice is soft and the liquid has thickened.

CARAMELIZED BANANA SLICES	*6*	*6*	*medium bananas, sliced*
	2 oz	*57 g*	*raw sugar*

Sprinkle the banana slices with sugar. Heat with a torch until the sugar is melted but not burned.

ASSEMBLY   *Caramel*
Mango purée

1. Place one large feuille de brick triangle flat with the top pointing forward. Stand another large triangle on top of it about 1 1/2" (3.8 cm) behind the point. Dip the two sides of a small right triangle in caramel and glue it behind and perpendicular to the upright triangle to hold it in place.

2. Fill the pastry shell with warm rice filling and place it in the center of a dessert plate. Fan a few caramelized banana slices over the filling and top it with a feuille de brick triangle assembly. Garnish the plate with caramelized banana slices and mango purée.

DOME OF WHITE CHOCOLATE MOUSSE WITH SERPENTINE OF CASSIS

STANTON HO

Executive Pastry Chef, *Las Vegas Hilton Hotel.*

Although the white chocolate mousse is a neutral flavor, notes Stanton Ho, the griottine cherries add the necessary flavor burst. "No sauce is needed to contradict the flavor," he says. "This is a great treat after a heavy meal, and it can be simple, production-wise. The serpentines can be made well ahead of time."

The dome sits on a coconut sablé cookie; the serpentine of cassis is something of a hybrid of fruit leather and tuile.

YIELD: 12 SERVINGS

Special Equipment:
Two half-sheet silicone mats
Twelve 2 3/4" (7 cm) diameter
Flexipan demi-sphere molds
Small hand brush or compressed air spray gun

BISCUIT JOCONDE			
5.75 oz	163 g	almond flour
5.75 oz	163 g	confectioners' sugar
2 oz	57 g	all-purpose flour
7.5 oz	213 g	whole eggs
7.5 oz	213 g	egg whites
1.5 oz	43 g	granulated sugar
4 tsp	8 g	dried egg whites
.25 tsp	1 g	cream of tartar
1.25 oz	35 g	unsalted butter, melted

1. Preheat oven to 400°F (204°C). Line two half-sheet pans with silicone baking mats.

2. In a bowl, combine the almond flour, confectioners' sugar, and all-purpose flour. Sift together twice.

3. In a mixer fitted with a whisk attachment, beat the eggs on high speed until doubled in volume.

4. By hand, fold in the sifted dry ingredients in three additions.

5. In the bowl of a mixer with the whisk attachment, combine the egg whites, one-third of the granulated sugar, the dried egg whites, and cream of tartar. Beat to soft peaks. Slowly add the remaining granulated sugar and beat until firm peaks form. Fold the meringue into the egg-flour mixture. Fold the melted butter into the mixture.

6. Spread the batter evenly onto the prepared pans and bake for 10 to 12 minutes until set and golden. Cool completely.

SERPENTINE OF CASSIS	1.5 oz	43 g	unsalted butter, melted
	3.5 oz	99 g	confectioners' sugar
	1.75 oz	50 g	cassis purée
	1 oz	28 g	all-purpose flour

1. Line 2 half-sheet pans with silicone mats. Have ready a rolling pin for shaping.

2. In a mixing bowl, combine all the ingredients and mix by hand to a smooth paste. Refrigerate for at least one hour.

3. Preheat the oven to 350°F (177°C).

4. Spread a thin layer of cassis paste on the prepared pans and bake for about 10 to 12 minutes. Do not overbake (the baked paste should be the color of the fruit). Let rest for one minute.

5. Turn the silicone mat with the baked paste onto parchment paper. While still warm and pliable, cut the paste into 24 "serpentinelike" triangular shapes. Wrap one end around the rolling pin. Cool.

Making the serpentine cookies.

WHITE CHOCOLATE MOUSSE	9 liq oz	266 ml	milk
	8.75 oz	248 g	white chocolate, such as Valrhona Ivoire, finely chopped
	.24 oz	6.7 g	gelatin sheets, softened in water
	4.25 oz	120 g	egg yolks
	1.5 oz	43 g	granulated sugar
	7 liq oz	207 ml	heavy cream, whipped to soft peaks

1. In a saucepan, bring the milk to a boil. Add the chopped chocolate, lower heat, and stir until the chocolate is melted. Add the drained gelatin to the melted chocolate and stir until dissolved. Remove from heat.

2. In a medium bowl, whisk together the yolks and sugar. Place the bowl over a hot water bath. Whisk the mixture to the ribbon stage.

3. Whisk the melted chocolate mixture into the egg mixture until combined.

4. Place the mixture over an ice bath and stir with a rubber spatula until it just begins to set. Remove the bowl from the ice bath and fold in one-third of the whipped cream. Fold in remaining whipped cream and chill.

| WHITE CHOCOLATE DOMES | 3 oz | 85 g | semisweet chocolate, tempered |
| | 9 oz | 255 g | white chocolate, tempered |

1. Freckle the tempered semisweet chocolate onto the Flexipan demi-sphere molds with a hand brush or a compressed air spray gun. Allow to set.

2. Place a thin, even coat of tempered white chocolate over the semisweet chocolate speckles to make a 1/16 to 1/8" (.16 to .32 cm) thick layer. Allow to set.

COCONUT SABLÉ COOKIES	11.5 oz	325 g	all-purpose flour
	2.75 oz	77 g	almond flour
	2.75 oz	77 g	flaked coconut
	.5 tsp	2.5 g	salt
	11.5 oz	325 g	unsalted butter, softened
	5.25 oz	149 g	confectioners' sugar
	1.75 oz	50 g	eggs

1. In a bowl, combine together the all-purpose and almond flours, coconut, and salt.

2. In a mixer fitted with a paddle attachment, cream together the butter and confectioners' sugar. Add the eggs and mix until incorporated.

3. On low speed, add the dry ingtredients to the creamed mixture, and mix until combined.

4. Shape the dough into a disc and refrigerate for at least one hour.

5. Preheat the oven to 375°F (191°C). Line a sheet pan with parchment paper.

6. Remove the dough from the refrigerator and roll out to 3/16" (.45 cm) thickness. Using a 3 1/4" (7.6 cm) fluted, round cutter, cut out 12 rounds of dough and place them on prepared pan.

7. Bake for 10 to 12 minutes, or until lightly browned. Cool on a rack.

| ASSEMBLY | 48 griottine cherries (about 3.75 oz /106 g)* |

*Note. Griottine cherries are available from Patisfrance, (800) PASTRY-1.

1. Cut out twelve 3 1/2" (8.9 cm) rounds from the joconde. Cut out twelve 1 3/4" (4.4 cm) rounds from the remaining joconde. Line demi-sphere molds with the larger round of joconde.

2. Pipe white chocolate mousse into the cake-lined molds. Arrange 4 griottines in each mold in a random fashion. Top with the smaller round of joconde. Refrigerate until set.

| ASSEMBLY | 48 griottine cherries (about 3.75 oz /106 g) |
| | Pulled-sugar sticks |

1. Place one coconut sablé cookie onto the center of a dessert plate.

2. Remove a mousse-filled mold from the refrigerator and unmold onto a coconut sablé. Arrange 4 griottines around the cookie.

3. Place a pulled-sugar stick onto the middle of the chocolate dome and garnish the plate with 2 cassis serpentines.

CHOCOLATE AND PEAR MOUSSE ENSEMBLE

ERIC PEREZ

Executive Pastry Chef, *Ritz-Carlton Tyson's Corners, Virginia.*

Chocolate, pear, and caramel are the classic flavor combinations at the core of this dessert, which Eric Perez has refined from a presentation that he frequently serves at the Ritz-Carlton in Virginia: chocolate and pear mousse with caramelized pears, layered in the middle, sits on a flourless chocolate biscuit. The dessert is encased by an almond pistachio biscuit. Caramel-pistachio ice cream is enclosed in the marbled chocolate sphere.

YIELD: 20 SERVINGS

Special Equipment:
Twenty ring molds, 3" (7.5 cm) diameter x 2" (5 cm) high
2" (5 cm) demi-sphere molds

CARAMELIZED PISTACHIOS

10.6 oz	300 g	whole pistachios
4 oz	113 g	granulated sugar
.5 liq oz	15 ml	water
.4 oz	12 g	unsalted butter

1. Slightly warm the pistachios in an oven. In a copper pot cook the sugar and water to 240°F (115°C). Add the nuts and stir until the mixture appears to crystallize. Continue cooking until the sugar melts and caramelizes evenly around the nuts. Quickly add the butter and mix well.

2. Pour the nuts out onto a silicone baking mat and separate each nut. Let cool.

ALMOND BISCUIT

10.5 oz	298 g	egg whites
4 oz	113 g	granulated sugar
3.5 oz	99 g	almond flour
3.5 oz	99 g	confectioners' sugar
1.8 oz	50 g	all-purpose flour, sifted
1.5 Tbs	22 ml	heavy cream
1.8 oz	50 g	caramelized pistachios, chopped

1. Preheat oven to 425°F (220°C). Spray 2 half-sheet pans with vegetable spray and line the bottoms with parchment paper. Whip 7.5 oz (213 g) of the egg whites to soft peaks while gradually adding the sugar. Combine the almond flour, confectioners' sugar, and flour; gently fold into the whites. Fold in the remaining 3 oz (85 g) of egg whites (unwhipped) and the cream.

2. Divide the batter into 2 half-sheet pans and spread evenly. Bake for 8 minutes or until the center springs back when gently pressed with a finger. Remove from the pans and cool completely.

CHOCOLATE BISCUIT	6 oz	170 g	Valrhona Pur Caraibe chocolate
	3 oz	85 g	unsalted butter
	10 oz	284 g	egg whites
	3.5 oz	99 g	granulated sugar
	2.5 oz	72 g	egg yolks

1. Preheat oven to 425°F (220°C). Spray a half-sheet pan with vegetable spray and line the bottom with parchment paper. Combine the chocolate and butter and melt over a double boiler.

2. In a mixer, whip the egg whites to soft peaks while slowly adding the sugar. Quickly incorporate the egg yolks and melted chocolate.

3. Spread the batter onto the prepared pan. Bake for 10 to 12 minutes or until the cake springs back when gently pressed with a finger. Remove from the pan and cool. (The cake will be extremely moist.)

CARAMELIZED PEARS	4	4	pears, cut into quarters and poached
	2.5 oz	71 g	unsalted butter
	4 oz	113 g	granulated sugar
			Poire William, to taste

1. Cut pears into 1/4" (.6 cm) slices and cut in half. Melt the butter in a large skillet. Add the pears and cook over medium heat, stirring, for about 5 minutes or until slightly softened.

2. Add the sugar and Poire William, with the pan off the heat, and mix well. Continue to cook, stirring, until the pears are caramelized but still firm.

CHOCOLATE MOUSSE	13 oz	369 g	Valrhona Pur Caraibe chocolate
	4 oz	112 g	egg yolks
	1.8 oz	50 g	eggs
	4 oz	113 g	granulated sugar
	3 liq oz	89 ml	water
	1 qt	946 ml	heavy cream, whipped to soft peaks

1. Melt chocolate over a double boiler and remove from the heat.

2. In a mixer on medium-high speed whip the yolks and the egg. While the yolks are whipping, cook the sugar and water to 244°F (118°C). Carefully pour the cooked sugar into the whipping eggs and increase to high speed. When foamy and light, reduce the mixer speed to medium and continue whipping until cool.

3. Gently fold the chocolate into the whipped cream. Fold the cream into the pâte à bombe.

PEAR MOUSSE	.4 oz	12 g	gelatin sheets
	2 liq oz	59 ml	Poire William
	16 liq oz	473 ml	pear purée
	2 oz	57 g	egg whites

3.5 oz	99 g	*granulated sugar*
2.5 liq oz	74 ml	*water*
16 liq oz	473 ml	*heavy cream, whipped to soft peaks*

1. Soften the gelatin in cold water. In a saucepan warm the gelatin and Poire William just until the gelatin melts.

2. Place the egg whites in a mixer fitted with the whip attachment. In a saucepan cook the sugar and water to 240°F (116°C), brushing down the side of the pan as needed. When the sugar reaches 230°F (110°C), start whipping the egg whites. The egg whites should reach soft peaks when the sugar is ready. Reduce the mixer speed and slowly pour in the cooked sugar. Increase the speed to high until the whites form stiff, shiny peaks, then reduce speed until cool.

3. Combine the melted gelatin and pear purée. Cool over an ice bath if it is still warm. Fold the meringue into the purée, then gently fold in the whipped cream.

WHITE CHOCOLATE CONES

| 8 oz | 227 g | *white chocolate, tempered* |

1. Make acetate cones 8" (20 cm) long with a 1" (2.5 cm) opening at the base. Coat the insides with the tempered chocolate and tap out the excess.

2. Let the chocolate set completely and remove the acetate.

CHOCOLATE TWISTS

| 8 oz | 227 g | *dark chocolate, tempered* |

1. Cut acetate into triangles 10" (25 cm) high with a 1" (2.5 cm) base. Spread with a thin coat of tempered chocolate and let it set just a little bit.

2. Wrap the triangle around PVC pipe 1" (2.5 cm) in diameter, forming a spiral about 8" long (20 cm). Let set completely and remove.

CHOCOLATE SPHERES

a few drops	a few drops	*Chefmaster oil-based red and green food coloring*
16 oz	454 g	*cocoa butter, melted*
6 oz	170 g	*dark chocolate, tempered*
12 oz	340 g	*white chocolate, tempered*

1. Add the red food coloring to half the cocoa butter and green food coloring to the other half. Spray 2" (5 cm) demi-sphere molds with the red cocoa butter. Let it set and spray with the green cocoa butter. Let set, again.

2. Splatter the molds with dark chocolate using a pastry brush. When the dark chocolate has set, coat the molds with white chocolate. Let set completely and unmold.

CARAMEL ICE CREAM

14 oz	397 g	*granulated sugar*
1 qt	946 ml	*milk*
1 qt	946 ml	*heavy cream*
10.5 oz	298 g	*egg yolks, beaten*
7 oz	198 g	*caramelized pistachios*

1. Cook the sugar until caramelized. Boil the milk and cream together and carefully add to the caramel off the heat. Temper in the egg yolks and cook to 185°F (85°C). Strain over an ice bath, cool completely, and refrigerate overnight.

2. Process in an ice cream machine according to the manufacturer's instructions. Add the caramelized pistachios to the ice cream as it is coming out of the machine.

CHOCOLATE SAUCE

20 liq oz	591 ml	water, divided
6.75 oz	191 g	granulated sugar
5 oz	142 g	bittersweet chocolate
1.5 oz	43 g	cocoa powder
.5 oz	14 g	cornstarch

1. Boil 16 liq oz (473 ml) of the water with the sugar. Add the chocolate and cook until completely melted.

2. Combine the cocoa powder, cornstarch, and remaining 4 liq oz (119 ml) of water. Temper into the melted chocolate and boil for 3 minutes. Cool.

CAKE ASSEMBLY

16 oz	454 g	dark couverture
16 oz	454 g	cocoa butter

1. Line the ring molds with acetate. Cut the almond biscuit into strips 9 1/2" (23.8 cm) long and 1" (2.5 cm) wide and line the ring molds. Cut the chocolate biscuit into 2 3/4" (6.9 cm) circles and place a circle in the bottom of each ring. Pipe pear mousse to fill half the mold, then top with a layer of caramelized pears. Pipe the chocolate mousse into the rest of the mold. Smooth the top and chill until set.

2. Melt together the chocolate and cocoa butter. Remove the cake rings from the freezer. While still frozen, spray the tops with the chocolate-cocoa butter mixture. Unmold.

DESSERT ASSEMBLY

White chocolate ribbons
Chocolate cigarettes
Poached Seckel pears

1. Attach the bottom of the chocolate twist to the base of the chocolate cone. Rub the base of the cone on a warm surface until it just starts to melt. Place on a dessert plate and let set.

2. Heat the tip of a knife or a small pastry tip and make a small hole in a chocolate demi-sphere. Place on the point of the cone. Fill the demi-sphere with caramel ice cream and top with another demi-sphere.

3. Place a mousse cake on the dessert plate. Top with a white chocolate ribbon. Garnish with a chocolate cigarette and a poached Seckel pear.

SWEET DREAM PARFAIT

SEBASTIEN CANONNE

Co-owner, *Ecole de Patisserie Francaise, Chicago.*

"This is the dessert we did for the World Pastry Cup in 1997," says Sebastien Canonne. *It is a bombe glace—strawberry sorbet, vanilla parfait, caramelized almonds, and almond dacquoise. Sautéed apricots in syrup are also part of the ensemble. The clock hand is formed with a honey wheat tuile, and the numbers are a chocolate mixture sprayed through a stencil. "The dome is like the actual clock, the cookie is the minute hand, the sugar wire is the second hand. It is time exploding,"* Canonne explains cryptically.

YIELD: 24 SERVINGS

Special Equipment:
Twenty-four 3 " (7.6 cm) demi-sphere molds
Wagner airless paint sprayer
Two 5/8 " (1.6 cm) diameter plexiglass modular molds
Clock-hand-shape template
Clock stencil

ALMOND DACQUOISE

9.5 oz	*270 g*	*TPT**
3 oz	*87 g*	*almond flour*
7.6 oz	*215 g*	*egg whites*
1.9 oz	*55 g*	*granulated sugar*

***Note.** TPT (tant-pour-tant) is a mixture consisting of 50% almond flour and 50% confectioners' sugar. You can make it by combining 4 3/4 oz (135 g) whole blanched semi-roasted almonds and 4 3/4 oz (135 g) confectioners' sugar in a food processor and grinding it to a fine powder.

1. Preheat the oven to 425°F (220°C). Combine the TPT and almond flour. In a mixer with the whisk attachment, whip the egg whites and sugar to soft peaks. Gently fold in the almond mixture.

2. Pipe the mixture into two 5/8" (1.6 cm) diameter Plexiglas modular molds. Smooth the tops, remove the molds, and bake for about 15 minutes or until just golden. If you do not have modular molds, spread the batter onto a parchment-lined half-sheet pan and after baking cut into two 1/2" (1.3 cm) circles.

CARAMELIZED ALMONDS	10.6 oz	300 g	whole almonds, lightly roasted
	4 oz	113 g	granulated sugar
	.5 liq oz	15 ml	water
	.4 oz	12 g	unsalted butter

1. **Sli**ghtly warm the almonds in an oven. In a copper pot, cook the sugar and water to 240°F (115°C). Add the nuts and stir until the mixture appears to crystallize. Continue cooking until the sugar melts and caramelizes evenly around the nuts. Quickly add the butter and mix well.

2. **Pour** the nuts out onto a silicone baking mat and separate each nut. Let them cool.

HONEY WHEAT TUILES	2.6 oz	75 g	unsalted butter (82%)
	3.9 oz	110 g	confectioners' sugar
	2.6 oz	75 g	lavender honey
	2.9 oz	83 g	egg whites
	3.9 oz	110 g	whole wheat flour
	1 tsp	5 g	ground ginger

1. **Pre**heat the oven to 325°F (160°C). In a mixer fitted with a paddle attachment, cream together the butter, confectioners' sugar, and honey. Add half the egg whites, then half the flour. Add the remaining egg whites and flour. Add the ginger, and mix just until combined.

2. **On** a sheet pan lined with a silicone baking mat, spread the batter in a thin layer through a clock-hand-shape template. Bake for 8 to 10 minutes or until set. Immediately place over a 1" (2.5 cm) diameter cylinder to shape.

STRAWBERRY SORBET	2.6 liq oz	77 ml	water
	3.7 oz	104 g	granulated sugar, divided
	2.1 oz	60 g	atomized glucose
	.5 tsp	2 g	sorbet stabilizer
	26.7 oz	756 g	strawberry purée (10% sugar)

1. **In** a saucepan, combine the water, 3.3 oz (94 g) of the sugar and the glucose. Bring to a boil and add the stabilizer mixed with the remaining .3 oz (10 g) of sugar. Return the mixture to a boil and immediately remove from the heat and cool. Chill for at least 3 hours.

2. **Combine** the syrup with the strawberry purée. Pass through a chinois and process in an ice cream machine according to the manufacturer's instructions.

VANILLA PARFAIT	12 liq oz	355 ml	heavy cream (35% butterfat)
	5.8 liq oz	172 ml	whole milk (3.6% butterfat)
	3 1/2	3 1/2	Tahitian vanilla beans
	4.9 oz	139 g	granulated sugar
	4.3 oz	123 g	egg yolks
	1.1 oz	31 g	inverted sugar

CHARTREUSE SUNDAE WITH MACADAMIA BROWNIES

PHILIPPE LAURIER

Executive Pastry Chef,
*Patisfrance USA, East Rutherford,
New Jersey.*

Philippe Laurier's mission was to take an American dessert and dress it up, European-style. He has accomplished this with a basic brownie, baking it in a teardrop mold and pebbling it with macadamia nuts and raisins macerated with Chartreuse and candied ginger, and crowning it with a dollop of Chartreuse ice cream. A florentine cookie with macadamias and chocolate tendrils round off the plate.

YIELD: 12 SERVINGS

Special Equipment:
Silicone baking mat
Curved triangular stencil 9" (22.8 cm) long x 6" (15.2 cm) high
Oval ring mold, 2 1/2 oz (70 g) capacity
Small gold-flecked transfer sheets

CHARTREUSE ICE CREAM

20 liq oz	591 ml	milk
7 liq oz	207 ml	heavy cream
1	1	vanilla bean, split and scraped
4.6 oz	130 g	egg yolks
7 oz	198 g	granulated sugar
1.5 liq oz	44 ml	Chartreuse liqueur

1. In a large saucepan, scald the milk with the cream and vanilla bean. Remove from the heat. Cover and allow to infuse for 1 hour. Discard the vanilla bean.

2. In a bowl, whisk together the egg yolks and sugar. Temper the yolks with the reheated milk mixture. Return to the saucepan and cook until thickened. Strain the custard and cool in an ice bath. Chill.

3. Process in an ice cream machine, adding liqueur during the last 5 minutes of churning.

MACADAMIA BROWNIE

1.5 oz	43 g	golden raisins
1.5 liq oz	44 ml	Chartreuse liqueur
3.5 oz	99 g	all-purpose flour
pinch	pinch	salt
1/8 tsp	1.8 g	baking powder
9 oz	255 g	unsalted butter, melted
7 oz	198 g	granulated sugar, divided
9 oz	255 g	bittersweet chocolate, finely chopped
.5 oz	14 g	crystallized ginger, finely minced
3.5 oz	99 g	lightly toasted macadamia nuts, finely chopped
3 oz	85 g	egg whites

CHAPTER FIVE

MODERNIST SAUCE PAINTING

LINCOLN CARSON

Pastry Chef,
*The Highlands Inn, Carmel,
California.*

BORN: March 1969,
Beirut, Lebanon.
TRAINING/EXPERIENCE: pastry
program, Johnson and Wales,
Rhode Island; Le Pactole, Le
Bernadin, Peacock Alley
(Waldorf-Astoria), Luxe, Four
Seasons Hotel, Cascabel, La
Côte Basque, all in New York.

*"I've had some lucky breaks. I
worked for some excellent people. I've
received a lot of great advice and
good training. Some of that training was under traditional French
management, which is based on fear.
I'm very serious about what I do,
but I'm not a screamer. My feeling
is, work harder than anyone working for you, and they'll do it for
you. Don't lose sight that there are
more outlets, creative and otherwise,
in your life. When you leave work,
leave work."*

Sauce paintings are an exquisite, accessible, affordable way to dress a dessert. The colors of sauces are so spectacular, and the colors of many main components are so drab,
that chefs will be tempted to choose sauces for their color rather than their flavor. "Don't,"
says Wayne Brachman of the Mesa Grill in New York. "One drop of sauce can radically
change the flavor of something. In the hands of a careful chef, each bite of a sauced dessert
will be slightly different, and all of them satisfying.

The Modernist chef has the option of making his or her own sauces from fresh fruit or making them from purchased, frozen purées—or both. "We keep fruit that is not perfect," says
Thomas Worhach of the Four Seasons Hotel in Palm Beach, Florida, "although berries
should be unblemished. Once a week we cook them, adding a little sugar. The sugar is
what helps preserve the fruit. Refrigerated, they will last two weeks, but the flavor really
is perfect only for a week, so we use them up in a week." Maintaining the sauces' consistency is not a problem, says Worhach. "We thicken it with cornstarch if we have to. You
don't want it too thick. You just want it to sit on the plate without the water running out."

"You want to leave the sauce as natural as possible," says Michael Hu of the Waldorf-
Astoria in New York. "Some sauces have a better consistency than others—cherry sauces
and other sauces with more sugar in them."

There are alternatives beyond those of purchased purées and conventional fruit purées.
Donald Wressell of the Four Seasons Beverly Hills does not consider sauce painting "the
forward motion" for many of his plate designs, but he is still intrigued by sauces. "I'm
becoming more interested in sauces that are clear rather than cream-based or purée-based,"
he says. "Burnt orange sauce is something I've evolved into. I like the look better. It fits
my plates better. I like reduction sauces too."

"Purées are a lot of work to do yourself," admits Thomas Worhach, "but a lot of these are
readily available now." Even chefs who make their own sauces will supplement their own
product with purchased purées. Improvements in shipping, manufacture, and customer
service have vastly improved the quality of these purées.

In the premium packaged brands, fruits are frozen as soon after harvesting as possible to
eliminate any degradation of color or flavor. No colorings or additives are used. A flash pas-
teurization process may be employed to control bacteria and oxidation once the purée is
defrosted. Many of the purées contain no added sugar, while a few do add some 10 percent
sugar. A knowledgeable chef can control the sweetness of each preparation.

Thomas Worhach is one of the acknowledged masters of this type of plate presentation; it
has become his signature. At banquets, he will try to arrange it so that every person at a
table will have a different sauce design around their dessert. It creates a sensation. This is
how it works in his kitchen:

Worhach always uses white plates. "Using showplates with all this saucing makes a plate
too busy," he says. Most of the time, his sauces are contained within a design piped in
chocolate with a paper cone. Worhach does every design free-hand. "I used to do free sauces,
twirling them, shaking the plate," he says, "but I wanted something a little more precise."
Why, then, does he go free-hand rather than employing templates? "I don't use anything
that could make it a perfectly designed sculpture"—in other words, Worhach feels that
much of the beauty in his designs lies in their inexactitude.

Worhach can do the chocolate lines well ahead of time. Then during service, he and other
members of his team will fill in the sauces. He puts the plate on a turntable and sauces the
broad areas with a squeeze bottle, then extends it into the fine area with a wooden pick. "I

don't want the dessert swimming in sauce. I want it only as part of the garnish," he says.

"The sauces can be done an hour ahead or so," he says. "They hold up that well." With Worhach doing the chocolate outlines and five of his people doing the saucing, it takes about an hour to do 110 desserts.

Modernists generally work clean, with sharp, distinct lines, though loose saucing is, of course, valid and beautiful. In this chapter we showcase the work of three chefs with three distinct approaches to saucing. "I have four people in my kitchen," says Lincoln Carson of The Highlands Inn in Carmel, California. "It's ludicrous for me to assume that every plate that goes out will be exactly like the way I'd put it out. It's important for them to get the style, the feel of the way I do things, but I tell them, play with it. I'm there during production, so I know the flavors will be there."

Here we have examples of the beauty of controlled sauce painting, as realized by Tom Worhach; looser saucing, as displayed by Lincoln Carson; and a third, hybrid style demonstrated by Wayne Brachman—precision saucing used to create an overall loose, freewheeling design. Any of these approaches can work, and additional sauce displays are seen throughout this volume.

Tom Worhach continues the triangular theme created by his Chocolate Almond Cappuccino Kaleidoscope—the slice is echoed by the triangles in the sauce painting. Tropical fruit purées are paired with the chocolate, almond, cappuccino flavor in the tart. In his Crispy Caramel Crab Apple Crysanthemum, the sauce portrait is in keeping with the floral/coral visual effect. Sauce flavors include mango, raspberry, papaya, and green apple. A floral theme accompanies his Kaffir Lime Tart. Mango, cactus pear, and kiwi coulis' match the lime tart flavor-wise and create an interesting color when blended.

Lincoln Carson chooses tequila orange sauce and cassis purée to accompany his Lemon Europa, a frozen lemon soufflé. The sauces echo the colors of the main ingredient and provide a nice planetary, galactic swirl to realize the theme that Carson had loosely in mind. (Europa is a moon of Jupiter where life might be found.) Caramel and chocolate sauces are arranged haphazardly around Carson's Hazelnut Mousse, in a brutal color combination. But, as was stated earlier in the book, the precision of the forms—Carson's mousse ring, the triangular cookies, the elegant coil of caramel—imply beauty and artistry in the loose saucing.

The flavors of these sauces blend beautifully with the main components. So how does that happen? "You can't intellectualize about flavor," says Wayne Brachman. He minimizes the importance of books, charts, and flavor wheels. "It is extremely primal," he says. "There's

THOMAS WORHACH

Executive Pastry Chef, *Four Seasons, Palm Beach, Florida.*

BORN: March 1952, Danville, Pennsylvania. TRAINING/EXPERIENCE: The Culinary Institute of America; Hotel Bel Air, Los Angeles; Ritz-Carlton Hotel, Houston; Ritz-Carlton Hotel, Philadelphia; Mansion on Turtle Creek, Dallas.

"Doing desserts for a book is one thing, to become a good pastry chef is another. Making desserts is just a small part of it, though it takes a lot of time. There's so much to learn—with the sugar, the chocolate, the baking, the banquet presentations. You have to be a good manager. You have to be respected, you have to know how to treat people, communicate with people. A good way to learn is to jump from job to job, see different environments, learn different styles and ways to do things. But it's also a good learning experience—and rewarding in itself—to build a relationship, to build a team."

WAYNE BRACHMAN

Executive Pastry Chef, *Mesa Grill and Bolo, both in New York.*

BORN: April 1951, Queens, New York. TRAINING/EXPERIENCE: various restaurants in New York and Massachusetts; Odeon, Arizona 206, both in New York. Author: *Cakes & Cowpokes* (William Morrow & Co., 1995).

"Pastry is one of the few jobs that almost works on a guild system, meaning old-fashioned standards of developing skills. It's mostly craft, but it has a smathering of artistry. The skill of what you're doing turns you on rather than the money. It had better because you're underpaid for what you do. You're in the production end, which never pays as much as sales. You work with waiters who get paid twice as much and don't need to care or take the work home. You will always be the back-up, the man or woman behind the executive chef. But you do it because you're driven, because you love it. Some jobs, you go into work, you sit in front of a computer and your life is on hold. But working in a kitchen is the same as living. It's aggravating at times, rewarding at times; you hang out, you work hard, but you keep communicating."

FROZEN HAZELNUT MOUSSE

LINCOLN CARSON

Pastry Chef, *The Highlands Inn,*
Carmel, California.

The frozen mousse is studded with truffle pieces and is served with a chocolate cookie. "With the caramel and chocolate sauces, there are a lot of reinforcing flavors on the plate," says Lincoln Carson. "It reminds me of an ice cream sandwich—crunchy on the outside, smooth and cool on the inside. Sometimes I'll make things and I'll start getting flavors reminiscent of my childhood or my family, and I'll go for that—there's got to be some reason why I'm remembering things from twenty years ago. There is something pleasant associated with it."

YIELD: 6 SERVINGS

Special Equipment: Six 5 oz (140 g) oval ring molds

CHOCOLATE TRUFFLE

10 oz	283 g	*bittersweet chocolate, finely chopped*
2 oz	57 g	*unsalted butter, cut into cubes*
8 liq oz	237 ml	*heavy cream*

1. Place chocolate and butter in a bowl. In a saucepan, bring the cream to a boil; slowly pour the hot cream over the chocolate and butter, whisking until the chocolate is completely melted.

2. Line a 9" (23 cm) square baking pan with plastic wrap. Pour in the truffle mixture. Freeze the truffle mixture until set.

3. Remove the truffle mixture from the pan and chop into 1/4 to 1/2" (.63 to 1.27 cm) pieces. Return the pieces to the freezer.

HAZELNUT MOUSSE

24 liq oz	710 ml	*heavy cream*
12 oz	340 g	*hazelnut paste (100% pure)*
2 liq oz	59 ml	*water*
8 oz	227 g	*granulated sugar*
6.5 oz	184 g	*egg yolks*

1. Line a sheet pan with parchment paper and place the oval ring molds on it.

2. In a mixer fitted with a whisk attachment, whip the cream to soft peaks. Add the hazelnut paste and whip to stiff peaks. Refrigerate.

LEMON EUROPA

LINCOLN CARSON

Pastry Chef, *The Highlands Inn, Carmel, California.*

Unremittingly lemon, this is a Meyer lemon semi-freddo with pieces of lemon inside and cassis sauce frozen on the outside, with cassis and orange tequila sauces in support. The lemon chips are lightly poached in sugar and dried. The lemon and cassis cookie reinforces the theme. "The name came to me the week that scientists discovered the possibility of life on Europa, a moon of Jupiter," says Lincoln Carson. "I thought that was extremely cool and this looked very planetary."

YIELD: 24 SERVINGS

Special Equipment: Twenty-four Flexipan 4 oz (118 ml) dome molds

BASE			
8 liq oz	237 ml	cassis purée
6	6	Meyer lemons
1 qt	946 ml	heavy cream
3.5 oz	99 g	whole eggs
3.25 oz	92 g	egg yolks
8 oz	227 g	granulated sugar

1. Pass the cassis purée through a fine chinois. Using a small brush, paint some of the cassis purée in a random design onto the interior of the dome molds, so that it beads. Freeze the molds to set the purée. Reserve the remaining purée to garnish the dessert plates.

2. Grate the zest of the lemons and reserve. With a sharp knife remove the lemon peels completely and cut out the individual lemon segments. Dice the lemon sections. Squeeze the juice from the remaining lemon membranes, and reserve.

3. In a mixer fitted with the whisk attachment, whip the cream to medium peaks. Add the lemon zest and whip to firm peaks. Reserve the whipped cream in the refrigerator.

4. In a mixer fitted with the whisk attachment, whip the eggs, egg yolks and sugar at high speed until tripled in volume. Fold the egg mixture into the whipped cream in two batches. Fold in the juice and the diced lemon segments. Fill the frozen dome molds with the lemon mousse. Freeze the molds for several hours, until hard.

LEMON SABLÉ	8 oz	227 g	unsalted butter
	8 oz	227 g	granulated sugar
	4	4	lemons, zested
	1	1	vanilla bean, split and scraped
	3.5 oz	99 g	whole eggs
	14 oz	397 g	cake flour

1. In a mixer fitted with the paddle attachment, cream the butter, sugar, lemon zest, and vanilla beans just until smooth. Beat in the eggs, scraping down the side of the bowl as necessary. At low speed, mix in the flour. Form the dough into a ball and chill the dough for at least 2 hours.

2. Preheat the oven to 350°F (175°C). Roll the dough out to 1/8" (.3 cm). Using a 4" (10 cm) round cutter, cut out 48 crescent shapes. Place half of the crescent shapes onto a silicone-lined sheet pan. Using the cutter, trim off the bottom third of the crescents. Places the remaining crescents on the pan and trim off the bottom two-thirds of these crescents. Bake until lightly browned, about 10 minutes.

LEMON CHIPS	6	6	Meyer lemons
	2 qts	1.9 lt	simple syrup
	3 oz	85 g	glucose

1. Slice the lemons very thinly. In a pan, combine the syrup and glucose. Add the lemon slices and gently poach them until they are translucent.

2. Preheat the oven to 220°F (105°C). Transfer the poached slices to a silicone baking-mat-lined baking sheet. Bake until crisp, 1 hour 45 minutes to 2 hours, turning the slices over occasionally.

TEQUILA-ORANGE SAUCE	1 tsp	2.5 g	cornstarch
	1 qt	946 ml	orange juice, divided
	2 oz	57 g	granulated sugar
	2 liq oz	59 ml	Sauza Commemerativo tequila

1. In a small bowl, dissolve the cornstarch in 2 Tbs (30 ml) of the orange juice; set aside.

2. Place the orange juice in a saucepan and bring to a boil over medium-high heat; boil the juice until it is reduced by half. Stir in the sugar.

3. Add the dissolved cornstarch mixture to the juice and bring it to a boil. Allow to boil for 1 minute. Remove the sauce from the heat and stir in the tequila. Chill.

ASSEMBLY

1. Unmold a frozen lemon soufflé onto a dessert plate. Pool some of the tequila-orange sauce around the dessert. Squeeze a random design of cassis purée onto the orange sauce.

2. Arrange a large lemon sablé and a smaller one on top of the dome, in a spiral pattern. Arrange 3 lemon chips on top of the dome. Repeat with the remaining soufflés and serve immediately.

KAFFIR LIME TART

THOMAS WORHACH

Executive Pastry Chef, *Four Seasons, Palm Beach, Florida.*

Although more aromatic than a Key lime, a Kaffir lime's flavor is delicate. Here, it is featured as a filling in a graham cracker crust, accompanied by coconut rum ice cream, passion fruit sorbet, mango and papaya slices, pineapple crisps, and cinnamon-coated, deep-fried angel hair pasta.

YIELD: 12 SERVINGS

Special Equipment:
Twelve 2" (5 cm) diameter × 1 1/8" (2.9 cm) high stainless steel ring molds
Silicone baking mat

COCONUT-RUM ICE CREAM

28 oz	794 g	Coco Lopez cream of coconut
20 liq oz	591 ml	milk
1 liq oz	30 ml	rum

1. Combine all the ingredients in a large bowl. Whisk until blended. Chill.

2. Process in an ice cream machine according to the manufacturer's instructions.

PASSION FRUIT SORBET

16 liq oz	473 ml	water
12 oz	340 g	granulated sugar
3 oz	85 g	glucose
32 oz	907 g	frozen passion fruit purée, thawed
2 liq oz	59 ml	lemon juice

1. In a large saucepan, bring the water, sugar, and glucose to boil. Remove from the heat and stir in the passion-fruit purée and lemon juice. Cool and chill.

2. Process in an ice cream machine according to the manufacturer's instructions.

PINEAPPLE CRISPS

7 oz	198 g	trimmed, peeled, whole pineapple
4 liq oz	118 ml	simple syrup

1. Preheat the oven to 150°F (66°C). Line a baking pan with a silicone mat.

2. Cut the pineapple into 12 very thin slices, about 1/16 to 1/8" (.16 to .32 cm) thick. If desired, remove the cores with a small cutter.

3. Brush both sides of the pineapple slices with simple syrup. Place the slices on the prepared pan and bake for 3 to 4 hours or until dry and crisp.

4. Transfer to a rack and cool completely.

GRAHAM CRACKER CRUST		
4 oz	113 g	graham cracker crumbs
2.25 oz	64 g	unsalted, roasted cashew nuts, finely ground
2.75 oz	78 g	granulated sugar
3 oz	85 g	unsalted butter, melted

1. Preheat the oven to 350°F (177°C). Line a baking pan with a silicone mat. Place the ring molds on a lined pan.

2. In a medium bowl, combine the graham cracker crumbs, ground nuts, and sugar. Stir in the melted butter and mix until well-blended.

3. Place about 2 to 3 tsp of crumb mixture into each ring mold and press down firmly to form a crust about 1/4" (.6 cm) thick. Bake for 6 to 8 minutes until golden and set. Let cool completely. Keep on the prepared pan.

KAFFIR LIME FILLING		
2.6 oz	74 g	egg yolks
16 liq oz	473 ml	sweetened condensed milk
4 liq oz	118 ml	fresh Kaffir lime juice (regular lime juice can be substituted)

1. Preheat the oven to 350°F (177°C).

2. In a bowl, mix the yolks and condensed milk until just combined. Add the lime juice and blend until smooth.

3. Fill the prepared molds with the lime mixture. Bake until set, about 20 minutes. Cool slightly at room temperature; unmold and chill.

MANGO AND PAPAYA SLICES	
3	ripe mangoes, about 10 oz (283 g) each
2	ripe papayas, about 12 oz (340 g) each

1. Peel the mangoes and thinly slice them on a mandoline.

2. Peel the papayas and thinly slice them on a mandoline.*

*Note. If this is being prepped ahead of time, arrange the slices, in one layer, on a tray lined with plastic wrap. Press the plastic wrap on top of the slices. Repeat the layering, separating each layer with plastic wrap. Chill.

ASSEMBLY

Mango coulis
Kiwi coulis
Cactus pear coulis
Deep-fried angel hair pasta drizzled with chocolate

1. Remove the lime tart from the refrigerator and place on a dessert plate painted with fruit coulis. Place one slice of pineapple crisp on top of the tart.

1. In a small saucepan, cook the raisins and the Grand Marnier until the raisins are plump.

2. In a large bowl, toss the crab apples with the lemon juice, cinnamon, vanilla, nutmeg, and brown sugar.

3. Melt the butter in a large sauté pan and sauté the apples until the sugar melts and the apples begin to soften. Off the heat, add the apple brandy. Return to the heat and continue to sauté until the apples are lightly caramelized, cooked through, but still firm.

4. Remove from the heat. Fold in the cooked raisins and walnuts. Set aside to cool.

VANILLA BEAN PASTRY CREAM			
4 oz	113 g	egg yolks
5.5 oz	156 g	granulated sugar, divided
1 oz	28 g	all-purpose flour
16 liq oz	473 ml	whole milk
1	1	vanilla bean, split and scraped

1. In a bowl, whisk together the egg yolks and 2.75 oz (78 g) of the sugar until smooth. Whisk in the flour to make a smooth paste.

2. In a saucepan, over medium heat, bring the milk, vanilla bean, and 2.75 oz (78 g) of the sugar to a boil. Remove from the heat and allow to steep for 30 minutes. Discard the vanilla bean.

3. Temper the yolks with half of the reheated hot milk mixture. Add the tempered yolks to the saucepan.

4. Continue cooking over medium heat, whisking continuously, until the mixture comes to boil. Cook for 1 minute. Cool over ice bath. Chill.

APPLE TUILES			
3	3	medium Granny Smith apples

1. Preheat the oven to 175°F (80°C). Line 2 half-sheet pans with silicone mats.

2. Peel and thinly shave the apples. Press the shaved apple onto the silicone mats. Bake until dry and crispy, about 3 hours. Cool.

3. Break into large pieces and store in an airtight container.

POACHED SPICED CRAB APPLES			
1	1	vanilla bean, split and scraped
1	1	whole nutmeg, cracked
2	2	3 " (7.6 cm) long sticks of cinnamon, broken
24 liq oz	710 ml	simple syrup
4 liq oz	118 ml	brandy
8	8	crab apples

1. In a large saucepan, bring all the ingredients except the apples to a boil. Reduce the heat and simmer for 15 minutes. Remove from the heat and strain.

2. Return the syrup to the saucepan. Bring to a boil and add the apples. Cook the apples in the simmering syrup until tender, about 5 to 7 minutes.

3. Cool the apples in the syrup.

1. Crack the coffee beans by lightly rolling over them with a rolling pin.

2. In a saucepan, scald the cream, milk, and cracked coffee beans. Remove this from the heat, cover, and allow to infuse for 1 hour. Strain through a chinois and discard the coffee beans.

3. Place the sugar and eggs in a bowl and whisk to blend. Temper the yolks with the reheated milk mixture. Return to the saucepan and cook until thickened. Strain the custard and cool in ice bath. Chill.

4. Process in an ice cream machine according to the manufacturer's instructions, adding the liqueur during the last 5 minutes of processing.

SPRAYED WHITE CHOCOLATE DIAMONDS			
	3 oz	85 g	bittersweet chocolate, tempered
	1 lb	454 g	white chocolate, tempered

1. Place the bittersweet chocolate in a small parchment cone and drizzle it randomly onto a small gold-flecked transfer sheet. Allow the chocolate to set.

2. Spread some of the tempered white chocolate over the dark chocolate drizzle in an even layer. Allow the chocolate to set slightly. Using the diamond template as a guide, cut out at least 24 diamond shapes with an X-acto knife. With both ends of a medium plain pastry tip, cut out a few circles from each diamond. Cut 8 of the diamonds in half vertically.

3. Using some of the tempered white chocolate, glue one diamond half onto each of the 16 whole diamonds (see photo on facing page). Allow the kaleidoscope garnishes to set completely.

ASSEMBLY

Melted dark chocolate
Assorted fruit purées
Sliced toasted almonds (15 to 18 per serving)
Gold leaf squares
Fresh raspberries
Mint leaf

1. Place some melted chocolate in a small parchment cone. Make a freehand outline of a star design on the dessert plates, leaving the center of the plate empty. Fill in the outlines with assorted fruit purées. Dip the sliced toasted almonds in melted chocolate so that 1/3 of each almond is covered with chocolate.

2. Unmold a mousse onto the center of a dessert plate and arrange some of the chocolate dipped almonds around the base of the dessert. Top with a small scoop of cappuccino ice cream. Gently drop a square of gold leaf over the ice cream (it should wrap around the scoop on its own).

3. Place a kaleidoscope garnish on top of the gold-wrapped ice cream scoop, pushing it gently into the ice cream so that it is secure. Garnish with a few raspberries and a mint leaf.

BUTTER PECAN CUSTARD CAKE

WAYNE BRACHMAN

Executive Pastry Chef, *Mesa Grill and Bolo, both in New York.*

Layers of pecan, angel food cake, and butter pecan custard are wrapped in a tuile flavored with mint and raspberry; the dessert is topped with fried rice vermicelli. Raspberry, mint, mango, and black sesame sauces accent the flavors of the dessert. "I use Chinese black sesame," says Wayne Brachman. "It has a toasty flavor rather than the sharp flavor of Goma." When he employs sauces, Brachman always uses a variety. "It's like some schools of Indian cooking, where every bite is supposed to taste different."

YIELD: 8 SERVINGS

Special Equipment: Eight ring molds, 3" (7.5 cm) diameter x 1 3/4" (3.3 cm) high

ANGEL FOOD CAKE			
8.5 oz	240 g	egg whites
1 tsp	2 g	cream of tartar
1 tsp	3 g	lemon juice
7 oz	198 g	granulated sugar, divided
.25 tsp	1 g	salt
2.25 oz	64 g	cake flour
1 tsp	4 g	vanilla extract
1 oz	28 g	toasted pecans, coarsely chopped

1. Preheat the oven to 325°F (165°C). In a mixer combine the egg whites, cream of tartar, and lemon juice and whip to soft peaks. Add 3.5 oz (99 g) of the sugar in a slow steady stream and continue whipping to stiff peaks.

2. Sift together the salt, flour, and remaining 3.5 oz (99 g) of sugar. Fold the dry ingredients into the egg whites, followed by the vanilla and pecans. Divide the batter evenly into eight ring molds on a parchment-lined sheet pan. Bake for 25–30 minutes or until the cake springs back when gently pressed with a finger. Cool and unmold.

CUSTARD			
24 liq oz	710 ml	heavy cream
6.3 oz	179 g	brown sugar
1.75 oz	50 g	granulated sugar
1 liq oz	30 ml	Myers's rum
1 tsp	4 g	vanilla extract
5.2 oz	147 g	egg yolks

CHAPTER **S** IX

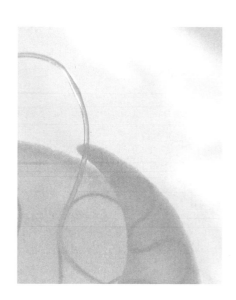

THE BUSINESS OF MODERNISM

Purchasing, costing, budgeting, menu writing: "You hear from students, 'I don't want to know about it. I don't give a damn. I just want to cook or bake,'" says Markus Farbinger of The Culinary Institute of America. "My reply is, 'That's fine. if you want to be a line cook all your life.'"

The fact is, the Modernist pastry chef must nurture experience in the management side of the business, if he or she ever dreams of running a kitchen. Readers who judge the desserts in this book as impractical will see that they can be quite profitable, if the kitchen that creates them is run efficiently.

In this chapter, three chefs from The Culinary Institute of America, Bo Friberg, Daniel Budd, and Markus Farbinger, have collaborated to create a dessert menu—it is menu-balanced to appeal to the largest number of potential customers; it is kitchen-balanced, to be feasible production-wise; and it is budget-balanced. The three CIA chefs then go on to explain the thinking behind this menu.

The skill we will focus on most closely here is costing. Other chefs will also put their two cents in, because all of the chefs in this book know the importance of management skills. Those of our chef-readers who are solidly in the weeds from the time they set foot in the kitchen until the time they schlep home will first want to know:

WHY SHOULD I LEARN COSTING PROCEDURES?

"Chefs must sometimes justify purchasing molds or ice cream machines or hiring new employees," says Markus Farbinger. "Without costing, you have no tool to show that you are profitable." The kind of thinking that costing inspires helps a young man or woman to think in terms of management. "With new equipment, you have to know what it will do for you; how much labor it will save; and how it can increase quantity, quality, and variety. How will it pay for itself? It's very important that you know these things, and that you can communicate them."

Even the most brilliant pastry kitchen can feel profitable, and not be. Stanton Ho of the Las Vegas Hilton checks and rechecks his costs—monthly, bi-monthly, weekly, sometimes daily. "It's not forced on me to do this," he says. "It's just something all chefs should do, rather than get carried away and think that they are free to do anything, then, at the end of the year, find that instead of making money, they are losing money."

Costing is just one skill among many that any ambitious chef should have. Markus Farbinger sings the praises of a bachelor's degree in pastry arts—or at the very least, for a chef to become interested in all phases of an operation. "Such a person will start out making the same base salary as the next guy, who had no training at all, but then you are able to understand the system beyond the stove, beyond the oven—sanitary, refrigeration, science of baking, interpersonal skills, design, understanding equipment. You should be able to take the hood off a malfunctioning Hobart and get some idea of how bad the situation is."

HOW DO I COST MY DESSERTS?

There are as many systems as there are styles of hotel and restaurant. Many large hotels have a system in place, with sheets providing a line-by-line template for how the institution wants its costs computed and displayed. Other restaurants may have no system at all, and management-ownership may feel it doesn't need one. "In smaller restaurants costing, figuring the labor costs down to the second, is not as important," admits Markus Farbinger. "The menu changes more often. You tend to go with the flow. In larger places, the menu doesn't change that often, and the chef tends to be there more."

At the Las Vegas Hilton, Stanton Ho and his kitchen staff must provide desserts and breads for more than eight restaurants, room service for a 3,000-room hotel, and banquet facilities that can seat 5,000 people at a clip. Not to scare the novice, but let's take a peek at Ho's costing procedure:

Like most chefs' systems, the costs will eventually be expressed as the cost per plate per dessert. The factors that go into this equation—in Stanton Ho's case, mind you—include ingredients (of course), the labor cost involved in mis en place, production (what an average person can do in a couple of seconds), and set up for service (down to the last berries on the plate, and the plates on the waiter trays); the cost of the plate itself (yes, the plate); timing and labor for every other procedure involved in getting the dessert from the kitchen to the customer and back again—from the waiters, busboys, and refrigeration staff who transport, maintain and serve the desserts to the stewards who clean the plates. Timing? "Yes, the timing," affirms Chef Ho. "Everything has to be timed here. By the time the dinner starts in a convention, everything must be plated. One hour and fifteen minutes before salad is served, you want all desserts finished and in refrigeration. The more you deviate from that formula, the more it costs." Transportation? Yes. At the Las Vegas Hilton, Stanton Ho's desserts might travel from a quarter to a half-mile to holding refrigeration, until they are served to the customers. "It's logistics," says Ho. "It's like plotting out a war game. That's what draws me to Las Vegas, the challenges necessitated by the volume. I learned by observing other chefs. Some of the best chefs in the world find endless time to fuss over dishes or buy the most expensive ingredients in the world. But this can make the difference between success and failure."

At the Waldorf-Astoria Hotel in New York, another high-volume, high-pressure operation, "Costing procedures are amazingly tight," says Michael Hu, the executive pastry chef. "We have to run 8 to 9 percent labor cost and an overall food cost of 21 to 22 percent. In order to do that, you have to run banquet food cost to 17 to 18 percent. It's easy to get bogged down by production alone. You have to manage yourself."

A more informal approach is taken by Donald Wressell, pastry chef at the Four Seasons Beverly Hills: "I don't cost every chocolate dessert because I know that every plated chocolate dessert is going to have upwards of three ounces of chocolate, maybe four, so I know the high end cost is going to be the chocolate," he says. "There's only so much cream, butter, eggs, and sugar we can cram on the same plate, so we came up with a generic cost for what a chocolate dessert would go for." The same situation exists for fruit desserts, ice creams, and so on. "We know where we stand with the ingredients we're working with," says Wressell. "We know how much a portion is going to cost.

"In the pastry kitchen," Wressell continues, "there aren't any ingredients in particular that are that outlandish. So I can go for a costly ingredient now and then. In the scheme of things, everything will balance out."

"The raw ingredient for a dessert is much less expensive than the raw ingredient for the hot kitchen," Norman Love of the Ritz-Carlton Hotel Company says. "Chocolate is an inexpensive ingredient." For this reason, if chefs want to spend a little more for an exotic ingredient for a special or a new seasonal item, they do not cut costs elsewhere. Rather than cut back on the quality of ingredients, some chefs will simplify the garnish.

DAN BUDD

Pastry Instructor,
*The Culinary Institute of America,
Hyde Park, New York.*

BORN: September 1967,
West Rutland, Vermont.
TRAINING/EXPERIENCE: The
Culinary Institute of America;
River Café and Park Avenue
Cafe, New York.

"I think that we should occasionally reflect upon our general appreciation for food and desserts, because I find that over time there are many things that make you happy, that you really like, and then there comes a point where you forget them. If you reflect back, not just on what you make but what you eat, it's always there for you to use for your benefit. {Executive chef} David Burke's food, and the experience of working with him, built an energy level in me, and built on my palate. It's an ongoing education, the building of knowledge for a chef."

MARKUS FARBINGER

Team Leader for Curriculum
and Instruction,
*Baking and Pastry Arts, The
Culinary Institute of America,
Hyde Park, New York.*

BORN: August 1964,
Taxenbach, Austria.
TRAINING/EXPERIENCE:
apprenticeship, Austria; Sacher
Hotel, Vienna; Amway Grand
Plaza Hotel, Michigan; Le
Cirque, New York City.

*"One of the major reasons that I'm
at the Institute is that it's a place
where you can influence the industry. I don't feel that I work for the
Institute, but for the industry, to
ensure that our profession will continue. At the school, we have the
responsibility to try new things, to
explore. The industry itself is busy
making money. They don't always
have time to try out new ingredients
and new equipment. We as a school
have a great responsibility to support, not just students, but research
and development."*

Most chefs, however, run costing procedures somewhere in between the Wressel informal-
ity and the Stan Ho exactitude. Most chefs break down the cost of making a single serving—ingredients plus labor. The variable is volume. Most chefs will be thinking in terms
of 20 or 30 portions nightly, but chefs in hotels will also need to consider whether the
dessert will be made in volume—for, say, a banquet for 500 people. In general, the higher the volume the lower the labor cost.

The price of raw ingredients will fluctuate also, but chefs deal with that in different ways.
Some chefs recost their desserts every year, to take into account changing costs of ingredients and labor. Thomas Worhach updates his costs weekly, but most chefs are more relaxed
on this issue; profits on desserts are so high, they say, that price fluctuations can be
absorbed.

The exceptions and caveats to this formula are endless. Bread, for example. That's a "hid-
den twist in your side," says Dan Budd, because it's a give-away. On labor: "I don't factor in labor," says Thomas Worhach. "Management doesn't care if it takes me three minutes or three hours. It's my time. I just report the actual cost of products." Norman Love
has a similar perspective in terms of labor: "You establish a standard, you enforce the
standard," he says. "You do not deviate from the standard. The standard becomes the
norm. If you demand perfection and never deviate from your expectations, what seems
like a difficult accomplishment becomes routine. Never sacrifice presentation because of
labor issues. Every plate must be perfect in every way, and if that requires a lot of work,
well . . ."

HOW DO I PRICE MY DESSERTS?

The formula most often cited to price the dessert is a simple one: set the price you charge
a customer at approximately three times your cost (not overhead; just ingredients and
labor). But there are other factors to consider.

Some chefs think of the 300 percent number as a starting point only; a minimum. They
then factor in "perceived value." This takes into consideration the environment that a
dessert is being served in (fine dining versus diner); the price of the entrées; the "wow"
factor of the presentation; and even the expectations of the customer—some banquet
clients will say the magic words, price is no object; their anticipation of the dessert will
heighten its value. There are desserts that are inherently easy to price up. As Dan Budd
says, when you sell a soufflé you're mostly selling air, but the perceived value of a soufflé
is very high.

"Pittsburgh's cost of living is relatively low," says Thaddeus Dubois of the Duquesne Club
there. "They were getting 4 dollars for desserts such as you see here [in this book]. Now
it's up to 6,7,8 bucks. Entrées were 18 to 26. I believe that desserts should be a third of
the entrées. I base it on that. Sales have actually gone up since the prices have gone up."

Some chefs believe that all the desserts on a menu should be priced the same; others disagree. Markus Farbinger has observed that management and chefs in small restaurants tend
to price desserts in accordance with a dessert already on the menu, pricing chocolate
desserts in one category, fruit desserts in another, and so on. "This is not wise for an item
that may be on the menu for a long time," he says.

"If there is more work involved, a higher price is justified," says Bo Friberg, "but you don't
inflate a price just because it is a best seller. That's the wrong way to go about it."

How do I balance my menu?

First, some anthropology: "When it comes time to look at the dessert menu, people are no longer hungry. You have a human animal that is fed and satiated," says Donald Wressell. "They don't need any more food. So you're appealing to an emotional reflex or whimsy or maybe something looks so good they have to have it. That's the real trick for the pastry chef. You have to entice someone into buying your product. I play into the emotional side—things that look really warm and inviting, but with very nice execution and attention to detail."

"On any menu you should have at least one 'wow' item," says Bo Friberg. "Something people will talk about. To compete today you must have that. You have to have one or two items with chocolate—a lighter one and a decadent, heavy one. You must have something with fruit, fresh, in season. You need to have something cold, an ice cream or sorbet. You need to have something on the lighter side. It's also nice to have a special of the day. This is also a good way to get rid of some waste. We're not talking about serving garbage. For example, if I have a banquet and maybe 75 of the people don't show up, I'm stuck with it. If it will hold up overnight—and only if—I might freshen it up and put it on special the next day.

"It never hurts to offer free items," adds Chef Friberg. "A little mignardise with the coffee. If the waiter can say, 'Something from the chef,' it makes the customer feel special, and it doesn't cost much."

"You don't need a huge menu," says Dan Budd. "If you can concentrate on a variety of things, six or seven items can be enough, and it gives you time to do them perfectly."

In the course of introducing new desserts on the menu, some will be money-losers, but that can have an upside too, says Dan Budd. "Money losers can be attention-getters," he points out. "The money loser might get the media. You might realize, this is costing me, but it's getting customers to come in and order desserts. So you have a sales factor, and media attention. Still, if they don't sell, you take them off the menu." Money losers will normally be balanced by winners. "Sorbets, for example. If you use fruits that are in season, you'll be making sorbet at two or three cents a scoop, the highest being 18 cents a scoop. You can sell three of those scoops for seven bucks. There are simple things you can do with less labor, like a soufflé. If you learn how to produce them efficiently, you can get good money for them.

"Chocolate is something you have to look out for," adds Budd. "It is the number one seller, but I've seen menus with too much chocolate. My students write menus, and they often do that."

When balancing a menu, according to Budd, "You have to relate to your customers, offer them their memories, things they're comfortable with." "You want to give them something they recognize," agrees Martin Howard of Rainbow! in New York. "I find it sells better if you give it a name they can recognize—chocolate chip, pie, a pudding, even if it's only a small portion of the dessert."

"I also believe that a customer needs to be able to relate to something on the menu," says Norman Love. "When you walk into a Ritz-Carlton in Atlanta, for example, you see a peach cobbler, something that people from that area are very familiar with. You want items that people from that area can relate to, and that visitors come to expect. You should have ingredients that are indigenous to the area. But it can be creative, totally dif-

BO FRIBERG

Chef Instructor, *The Culinary Institute of America at Greystone, St. Helena, California.*

TRAINING/EXPERIENCE: apprenticeship, Sweden; pastry school, Sweden (earned European Master Chef certificate); Sweden House Bakery, Tiburan, California; various cruise ships. Author: *The Professional Pastry Chef* (Van Nostrand Reinhold, 1996).

"For me, respect, a love of what you're doing, determination to learn, experience—these are what make a succesful pastry chef. When you enjoy what you're doing, you do a better job, rather than doing it as just a job. You want respect from your peers, or your students if you are a teacher. Part of this is showing them also that, yes, I make mistakes. That makes them feel better, gives them confidence. There is much to be said for experience, and unfortunately experience comes with age. It's taken me forty years of cooking pastries to write that book. Oh, and one more thing helps to make a succesful chef—pure luck. Sometimes it's just being in the right place at the right time."

ferent from a traditional concept, as long as the traditional concept is implied in the printed menu."

The recipes in this chapter reflect what the CIA chefs consider to be a good, balanced menu. Balanced, in the sense of variety to offer every customer as well as varying degrees of difficulty for the kitchen, in terms of production.

The menu includes three desserts that feature fruit, one of which (Apple Pie Soufflé) is apple, which is always a best-selling item, and another which is emphatically calorie light (Thin Ice Fruit Soup), an option that every menu should offer. Two items, excluding the mignardise, contain chocolate, a must, it goes without saying. These items, Mount Peppermint and Chocolate Marquise, are in the "decadence" category, where many customers like to visit. Four of the menu items contain a prominent vertical component, which many chefs believe has customer appeal and will help sell dessert items. Two of the items are relatively easy (and inexpensive) to produce in an average pastry kitchen—Thin Ice Fruit Soup and Mount Peppermint—while the Chocolate Marquise and Blueberry Financier, with all their garnishes, would be more labor intensive and, therefore, more expensive. Apple Pie Soufflé is inexpensive to produce but, like all soufflés, is tricky to make and requires someone in the kitchen with experience. Also included is an ultramodern mignardise presentation, which is generally offered gratis to preferred customers. The good will such a presentation generates cannot be calculated, nor can it be measured in any bottom line way, but experienced restauranteurs will attest that such premiums are crucial to a long-term business strategy.

A closer look at some of the prominent features of these desserts:

Thin Ice Fruit Soup is not only the ultimate light experience, but Markus Farbinger designed it to be a digestif, with the careful blending of herbs that he prefers for that purpose. It's a good option for waiters to offer to diners who clearly have already had too much of a good thing.

A marquise is normally, but not always, prepared in a loaf pan, but Chef Friberg has given his Chocolate Marquise a vertical dimension by preparing it in a PVC pipe; when unmolding, he measures standard lengths and cuts in alternate 45 then 90 degree angles, to give it a distinctive look. His Blueberry Financier is a lighter, custard-ish experience, but its simplicty is enhanced with the attention-getting, sweeping, and interlocking crescent cookies. Dan Budd's Mount Peppermint, a frozen peppermint mousse, offers the menu a rich option, mint, chocolate, and a vertical presentation, with both crunchy and smooth components on the plate. Budd's Apple Pie Soufflé has a crunchy apple texture and an eye-catching appearance with the garnish of poached, julienned apples, which of course can be made in bulk well ahead of time.

The mignardise presentation is somewhat outlandish, but that adds to its appeal in many settings. It has a deco, very modern appearance. The spicy chocolate dipping sauce is a welcome, unique addition—much talked-about afterward. Good food, good business.

WHAT OTHER MANAGEMENT CONSIDERATIONS ARE THERE?

Plenty. Most of it you will not learn in books, only in the field. Here, however, is a field guide:

Consider Quality Shortcuts. The quality of frozen fruit purées, chocolate cups, mixes, and other products has risen over the past decade. Most chefs agree, you do whatever it takes to get the job done. "In the last few years, the quality of ready made products has increased a great deal," says Markus Farbinger. "The companies seem to listen now to chefs, not just present a product without testing it. The fruit purées are fruits picked at the peak of their flavor. What can be better than that?"

Bo Friberg agrees. "I can be totally pure, use only the fresh stuff and wind up in the poor house. To compete, you have to compromise now and then. You don't use bad products like canned fruits, but the fruit purées are good. Some puff pastry and halfway products like florentine mix, the customer cannot tell the difference. If it tastes just as good and cuts down the cost by more than half and it can be stored on the shelf, why shouldn't you? In an emergency, if you have to, you purchase from the outside. You should draw the line if convenience is the only factor. If it doesn't have the right consistency or flavor you don't use it."

Organization, Refrigeration, Sanitation. "Much of a successful kitchen is proper storage and planning," says Bo Friberg. "'Freezer' used to be a dirty word. But if you know how to use it correctly, with things that don't break down, you can save a lot of time." Knowledge of refrigeration and storage is a very important skill to have, adds Friberg. "Some things you can take out of the freezer, let thaw, divide it in half, and put the other half back," he says. "Other things you absolutely cannot do that with. You have to know the difference. Anyone who is running a department should have a sanitation degree, so he or she can know what can be done. Certain things are against the law: raw eggs, for example. You still see them in recipes. You need to pasteurize the egg whites."

Developing Relationships with Purveyors. Once chefs are satisfied with their purveyor network, they tend not to shop around. "Competitive pricing is an issue, but not the most important one," says Norman Love. "You want dependability too. You don't shop around and switch purveyors to save twenty cents on a block of chocolate. You build relationships, based on the quality of the product and the service level they provide. The only thing you shop around for are unusual products. Pop-ups and banquets occur, and put the pastry chef in a bind, and the purveyor will bail them out sometimes. 'I need two more flats of strawberries. I need another case of chocolate cups.' These sorts of things are always occuring. It's the loyalty, the relationship, the level of surface, and the ingredients that are the most important thing."

People Skills. "The days of the screaming chefs are gone," says Michael Hu. "People are realizing that they can't do it alone. They're only as good as their staff. If you don't have those skills, people won't work for you."

In summary: "You have to be a hard worker," says Michael Hu. "If you're not, in this industry, you'll never survive. But it's not enough to be a hard worker. You have to be a smart worker. You have to know how to empower people and to pass the baton, give people the chance to prove themselves. They'll make mistakes, but you have to know to be there."

So many things to know, for the Modernist, the manager, the chef; the genius with flavor; the Rembrandt of color, composition, and surface texture; the simultaneous rule-breaker, and classicist; the people person, and the moody iconoclast.

The way of the Modernist is never easy. But the rewards are great. Not just the satisfaction of a job well done, a happy customer, a modest pay check, and the esteem of colleagues. No. Something more: immortality.

"In the future," Wayne Brachman predicts, "every dessert will be famous for fifteen minutes."

MOUNT PEPPERMINT

DAN BUDD

Pastry Instructor, *The Culinary Institute of America, Hyde Park, New York.*

The classic flavor combination of chocolate and mint is featured in a frozen peppermint mousse with chocolate chips and a peppermint chip brownie. The plate, by design, exhibits several shades of green, including sprayed white chocolate colored with green and a sugar mint leaf. "Like many people I over-did mint sprigs on desserts," admits Dan Budd. "In the modern age, I thought maybe I'd make a mint garnish myself."

YIELD: 15 SERVINGS

Special Equipment: Cone-shaped paper drinking cones

FROZEN PEPPERMINT MOUSSE			
3 oz	85 g	granulated sugar
3 liq oz	89 ml	water
4	4	mint tea bags
2.6 oz	74 g	egg yolks
1 liq oz	30 ml	crème de menthe
1/2 tsp	1 g	peppermint oil
12	12	mint leaves, finely chopped
28 liq oz	828 ml	heavy cream, whipped to soft peaks
1/4 tsp	.5 g	green liquid food coloring
8 oz	227 g	bittersweet chocolate, chopped into chips

1. In a saucepan, combine sugar and water; bring to a boil. Remove the pan from the heat, add the tea bags, and allow to steep.

2. In mixer fitted with a whisk attachment, beat yolks at high speed. Remove the tea bags from the sugar syrup, return the syrup to a boil, and then pour the hot syrup onto the whipping yolks. Continue beating until the yolks are fluffy and cool. In a bowl, combine the crème de menthe, peppermint oil, mint leaves, whipped cream, and food coloring. Gently fold the mixture into the yolks. Fold in the chocolate chips into the mixture and divide the mousse among fifteen paper drinking cones, filling them completely. Stand the cones upright in a sugar-filled hotel pan and freeze for at least 4 hours, but preferably overnight.

Dessert shown on page 218.

PEPPERMINT CHIP	10 oz	283 g	bittersweet chocolate, chopped
BROWNIES	10 oz	283 g	unsalted butter
	12 oz	340 g	cake flour
	.5 tsp	3.5 g	salt
	12 oz	340 g	light brown sugar
	12 oz	340 g	granulated sugar
	15	15	mint leaves, finely chopped
	10.5 oz	298 g	whole eggs, at room temperature
	.5 tsp	1 g	peppermint oil
	.5 oz	14 g	vanilla extract
	12 oz	340 g	bittersweet chocolate, chopped into chips

1. Preheat oven to 350°F (175°C). Line a half-sheet pan with buttered parchment paper. In a double boiler, melt together the 10 oz of chopped bittersweet chocolate with the butter; set aside.

2. In a bowl, sift together the cake flour and salt; set aside.

3. In mixer bowl, stir together the brown sugar, granulated sugar, and mint leaves. Add the eggs and whisk over simmering water until the mixture is just warm. Place the bowl in the mixer stand, and using the whisk attachment, beat at high speed until light and fluffy. Fold in the chocolate mixture, peppermint oil, and vanilla. Fold in the flour mixture and then the chips.

4. Pour the mixture into the prepared pan and bake until set but still soft, about 30 minutes Cool the brownies completely and then cut into rounds that are slightly larger than the bases of the paper cups.

CHOCOLATE SAUCE	12 oz	340 g	semisweet chocolate, finely chopped
	12 liq oz	355 ml	heavy cream
	4 oz	113 g	light corn syrup

1. Place the chocolate in a mixing bowl. In a saucepan, bring the cream and syrup to a boil and pour over the chocolate.

2. Stir until the chocolate is completely melted. Serve warm.

ASSEMBLY

Fresh mint sprigs
Peppermint-leaf sugar stems
Green leaves airbrushed onto plate

1. Place a brownie round in the center of a decorated dessert plate. Unmold a frozen peppermint mousse cone onto the brownie.

2. Pour chocolate sauce around the brownie just at the base of the cone. Stand a peppermint sugar stem into the frozen mousse.

> *"In a restaurant atmosphere it's sometimes difficult to make garnishes," admits Dan Budd. "This mint sprig is not difficult to make. You pull out long pieces of warm sugar and cut them into small pieces with scissors; that's the stems. You pull a lot of leaves—I flavor mine with peppermint extract—and store them away. Then, every day, you take out some stems and leaves, warm up the leaves and stick on a day's worth of stems."*

APPLE PIE SOUFFLÉ

DAN BUDD

Pastry Instructor, *The Culinary Institute of America, Hyde Park, New York.*

"I like to do things that relate to what people know about or already want," says Dan Budd. *"Apple pie is one of the best-selling desserts there is. So I tried to take the components of apple pie and do it in a more modern way. Then we added an element of another type of dessert that sells well, a soufflé. The best apple pie is a hot one, anyway. For service, the dessert works well. It's baked in the same dish, so it's sure to go out hot. Like a pie, the crust holds in the moisture."*

YIELD: 12 SERVINGS

Special Equipment:
Pinstripe-textured rolling pin
3" (7.6 cm) diameter x 2" (5 cm) high metal cake rings
3" (7.6 cm) diameter shallow pie dishes
3" (7.6 cm) dome molds or cut-off ladles

CRÈME FRAÎCHE ICE CREAM		
1 qt	*946 ml*	*milk*
1 pt	*473 ml*	*heavy cream*
14 oz	*397 g*	*granulated sugar, divided*
2	*2*	*vanilla beans, split and scraped*
2 tsp	*4 g*	*grated lemon zest*
11.7 oz	*332 g*	*egg yolks*
1 lb	*454 g*	*crème fraîche*

1. In a saucepan, combine the milk, cream, half of the sugar, vanilla bean seeds, and lemon zest. Bring the mixture to a boil; remove from the heat.

2. In a bowl, whisk together the yolks and the remaining half of the sugar. Add some of the hot liquid to the yolks to temper them and pour the entire mixture into the saucepan. Cook over medium heat, stirring constantly, until the mixture coats the back of a spoon. Immediately strain the mixture into a bowl set over an ice bath. Stir until cold.

3. Fold in the crème fraîche. Process the mixture in an ice cream machine according to the manufacturer's instructions.

CRUST		
8 oz	*227 g*	*granulated sugar*
1 lb	*454 g*	*unsalted butter, softened*
1 tsp	*2 g*	*finely grated lemon zest*
3.5 oz	*99 g*	*whole eggs*
2 tsp	*8 g*	*vanilla extract*
1.5 lbs	*680 g*	*all-purpose flour*

1. In a mixer fitted with a paddle attachment, beat together at high speed the sugar, butter, and lemon zest until smooth and creamy. At medium speed, add the eggs and vanilla. At low speed, mix in the flour just until combined. Pat the dough into a round, wrap well, and chill for 2 hours.

2. Divide the dough into two parts. Roll each part into a 12" (30 cm) X 17" (43 cm) sheet, 1/4" (.6 cm) thick. Using the textured rolling pin, roll pinstripes into the dough lengthwise. Layer the sheets between parchment paper and chill thoroughly.

3. Using a pastry wheel, cut the textured dough into twelve 2" (5 cm) X 10" (25 cm) strips. Wrap the strips around the ring molds, pressing the dough together at the seams to seal. Chill the prepared rings well.

4. Preheat a convection oven to 350°F (175°C). Bake the rings until lightly golden, about 20 minutes.

APPLE CHIP GARNISH			
	16 oz	*454 g*	*granulated sugar*
	16 liq oz	*473 ml*	*water*
	1 liq oz	*30 ml*	*lemon juice*
	1	*1*	*cinnamon stick*
	12	*12*	*Granny Smith apples*

1. In a saucepan, combine sugar, water, lemon juice, and cinnamon stick. Bring to a boil, stirring until the sugar is dissolved, and remove from heat.

2. Preheat oven to 180°F (82°C). Peel and core the apples and cut them into a julienne (2 x 1/8 x 1/8" / 5 x .3 x .3 cm). Add the apples to the syrup and gently stir until the apples become limp. Strain the apples and cool. Spread a thin lacy layer of apples into a circle on a Silpat mat. Bake until the chips are dry, about 2 hours. Remove the chips from the oven, and, before they are cool, mold them over a 3" (7.6 cm) diameter dome mold to create cage shapes. Store in an airtight container before serving.

Making the apple chip garnish.

APPLE FILLING			
	8	*8*	*Granny Smith apples*
	8 oz	*227 g*	*granulated sugar*
	1 liq oz	*30 ml*	*lemon juice*
	8 oz	*227 g*	*unsalted butter*
	4 liq oz	*118 ml*	*apple liquor*

1. Peel and core apples and cut into a large dice (1/2 x 1/2"/1.3 x 1.3 cm).

2. In a small bowl, blend the sugar and lemon juice together. Heat a large sauté pan and add the sugar mixture. Cook to a golden caramel; add the butter and stir to combine. Add the apple dice and sauté until slightly soft and caramelized. Remove the pan from the heat. Add the apple liquor, return to the heat, and flambé. Cook the apples until the flame dies and the alcohol is burned off. Pour the filling into a container and cool.

3. Place 2 to 3 oz (56 to 85 g) of the filling into the bottom of each pie dish and place the prebaked rings over the filling.

APPLE SOUFFLÉ			
	27 oz	765 g	granulated sugar
	8 liq oz	237 ml	water
	1/4 tsp	.7 g	cream of tartar
	.5 oz	14 g	ground cinnamon
	20 oz	567 g	applesauce
	15.75 oz	446 g	egg whites

1. Preheat the oven to 350°F (175°C). In a large heavy bottomed saucepan, combine the sugar, water, and cream of tartar. Cook to 240°F (115°C). Add the cinnamon and applesauce, and continue cooking.

2. At this point, in a mixer fitted with a whisk attachment, begin to whip the whites. When the applesauce mixture reaches 220°F (104°C), steadily pour it into the whites while continuing to whip to soft peaks, (do not overwhip). When the whites form soft peaks, and while the meringue is still warm, pipe the mixture into the rings of dough over the filling to the top of the ring. Bake the rings for 15 minutes, or until slightly risen and golden on top.

3. Sprinkle each soufflé with confectioners' sugar, top with an apple chip, and serve hot with crème fraîche ice cream on the side.

THIN ICE FRUIT SOUP

MARKUS FARBINGER

Team Leader for Curriculum and
Instruction, *Baking and Pastry Arts,*
The Culinary Institute of America,
Hyde Park, New York.

This dessert was inspired by a beautiful, familiar wintertime sight: when shallow ponds of water freeze, the unfrozen water, grass, and stones are visible just beneath the surface. From this Chef Farbinger has created a digestif— fresh fruit in a pool of half-frozen soup. The infusion can be anything that pleases your palate, but Chef Farbinger recommends herbs that aid digestion and freshen breath—lemongrass, fennel, pink pepper, coriander. This version includes lemonbalm, red peppercorns, vanilla beans, and sugar. Lemon and orange skin has been added to enhance the fruit flavors. The ratio of 20 percent sugar to water ensures that the soup will not freeze entirely.

YIELD: 24 SERVINGS

32 liq oz	*946 ml*	*water*
7 oz	*198 g*	*granulated sugar*
1 strip	*1 strip*	*orange peel*
1 strip	*1 strip*	*lemon peel*
1	*1*	*vanilla bean, split*
1 bunch	*1 bunch*	*lemonbalm or mint*
3	*3*	*red peppercorns, crushed*
1 liq oz	*30 ml*	*lemon juice*
2	*2*	*oranges*
2	*2*	*nectarines*
1	*1*	*pineapple*
2 oz	*57 g*	*grapes*
2	*2*	*mangoes*
4	*4*	*kiwis*

1. In a saucepan, combine water and sugar and bring them to a boil. Remove the pan from the heat and add the citrus peels, vanilla bean, lemonbalm, and peppercorns. Cover the pan and allow the mixture to infuse for 1 hour.

2. Transfer the mixture to a container and refrigerate for at least 8 hours; strain and stir in the lemon juice.

3. Peel the oranges and cut into segments. Cut the nectarines off the pits and slice thinly. Peel and core the pineapple and cut it into 1/8" (.3 cm) slices. Cut each slice into 1" (2.5 cm) wedges. Cut the grapes in half. Peel the mango and kiwis and cut into 1/8" (.3 cm) slices. Cut each slice into 1" (2.5 cm) wedges.

4. Place all the prepared fruit in a bowl. Pour over the chilled infusion. Refrigerate until ready to assemble.

ASSEMBLY   *Lavender*
Elderberry blossoms
Johnny Jump-ups

Pour about 8 liq oz (237 ml) of the fruit soup in each serving bowl. Sprinkle with the flowers. Freeze for about 1 hour before service. (The surface of the soup should be frozen.)

HOT CHOCOLATE WITH MIGNARDISES

MARKUS FARBINGER

Team Leader for Curriculum and Instruction, *Baking and Pastry Arts, The Culinary Institute of America, Hyde Park, New York.*

This is a Modernist take on the old favorite, chocolate fondue, paired with mignardises. The chocolate dipping sauce is served warm, but the heat comes from the red jalapeño peppers and the spices. The mignardises are caramel grapes, with their bottoms dipped in chocolate, and honey-roasted peanuts; almond batter friandises with brandied cherries; sesame leaf croquant, which is folded into caramel; and orange and coffee flavored tuiles.

YIELD: 16 SERVINGS

Special Equipment:
Eighty-five 1" (2.5 cm) diameter x 3/4" (1.8 cm) high aluminum or paper cups
Binder clips

COFFEE-ORANGE TUILES	8.8 oz	250 g	granulated sugar
(YIELD: 72 PIECES)	8.8 oz	250 g	sliced almonds, finely chopped
	.8 oz	25 g	coffee beans, coarsely ground
	2.6 oz	75 g	pastry flour
	7 oz	198 g	unsalted butter, melted
	1	1	orange, zested and juiced

1. Preheat oven to 375°F (190°C). In a bowl, combine the sugar, almonds, coffee beans, and pastry flour. Stir in the melted butter, orange zest, and juice.

2. Spoon out .3 to .4 oz (10 to 12 g) balls of the batter onto a Teflon sheet pan. Flatten each ball with a fork to form a round disc. Bake until golden, about 10 minutes. Cool slightly and shape as desired. Store in an airtight container until serving.

LEAF KROKANT STICKS	5 oz	142 g	almond flour, toasted
(YIELD: 75 PIECES)	2 oz	57 g	sesame seeds, lightly toasted
	1	1	vanilla bean, split and scraped
	2 oz	57 g	confectioners' sugar
	10 oz	283 g	granulated sugar
	1 Tbs	15 ml	lemon juice

1. In a food processor, place the almond flour, sesame seeds, vanilla bean scrapings, and confectioners' sugar. Process until just slightly oily, about 30 seconds.

2. In a heavy saucepan, combine the granulated sugar and lemon juice; cook over medium-high heat until it becomes a medium-brown color. Immediately pour the hot sugar onto a silicone baking mat-lined sheet pan. Spread the caramel into an even rectangle. Sprinkle about one-third of the almond flour mixture over the rectangle. Carefully fold the puff pastry into a rectangle as you would for a letter, in thirds. Roll out to another rectangle and sprinkle with another third of the almond flour mixture. Fold in thirds again. Repeat with the remaining flour mixture. Roll out to 1/4" (.6 cm) thickness and, while still warm and using a caramel cutter or sharp French knife, cut into 3/8 x 2 1/2" (.9 x 6.3 cm) slices. Store in an airtight container until service.

SOUFFLÉS FRIANDISES GRIOTTINES (YIELD: 85)			
8.5 oz	241 g	almond flour
6 oz	170 g	granulated sugar
.25 tsp	1.6 g	salt
1 oz	28 g	cornstarch
1 tsp	2 g	grated lemon zest
6 oz	170 g	egg whites
2 oz	57 g	honey
5 oz	142 g	unsalted butter, melted and browned
42	42	brandied cherries, cut in half

1. Spray 85 aluminum or paper cups (1" / 2.5 cm diameter x 3/4" / 1.8 cm high) with nonstick cooking spray. Preheat oven to 350°F (175°C).

2. In a bowl, combine the almond flour, sugar, salt, and cornstarch. Whisk in the egg whites, honey, and browned butter until well-blended. Spoon about 1/4 oz (8 g) of batter into each of the prepared cups. Place half of a brandied cherry in each cup. Press down on each cherry lightly, submerging it slightly. Bake for 8 minutes, until puffed. Dust with confectioners' sugar and serve warm.*

*Note. Batter-filled cups may be kept in the refrigerator or freezer and baked when needed.

CARAMELIZED GRAPES			
60	60	grapes, with stems
1 pt	.47 lt	water
3 lbs	1.36 kg	granulated sugar
4 oz	113 g	glucose
8 oz	227 g	bittersweet chocolate, tempered
8 oz	227 g	lightly salted peanuts, toasted

1. Trim the grape stems so that there is 1/2" (1.3 cm) of stem attached to each grape. Attach each grape stem to a binder clip. Place about 10 long skewers on the edge of a table, so that they extend beyond the edge of the table. Secure them by placing a heavy object on top of them on the table. Cover the floor area around the skewers with newspaper.

2. In a heavy saucepan, combine the water and sugar. Bring the mixture to a boil; stir in the glucose and cook the syrup to 300°F (149°C). Remove the pan from the heat.

3. Dip each grape halfway into the caramel. Hang each grape on the skewers, so that an "antenna" forms from the dripping caramel.

4. When cool, trim the antennae to 2" (5 cm) with scissors. Remove the clips and the stems from the grapes.

5. Dip the exposed end of each grape into the tempered chocolate. Immediately place the chocolate end of the grape in the chopped peanuts. Allow the grapes to set completely.

DIPPING SAUCE			
17 liq oz	503 ml	milk
1	1	vanilla bean, split
.7 oz	21 g	honey
pinch	pinch	salt
25 oz	700 g	El Rey Extra Amargo chocolate, melted
3.5 oz	100 g	unsalted butter, softened
1	1	ripe jalapeño (red), seeded and minced

1. In a saucepan, combine the milk, vanilla bean, honey, and salt. Bring the mixture to a boil. Remove the pan from the heat, cover, and allow to infuse for 10 minutes.

2. Remove the vanilla bean and pour the hot milk mixture over the melted chocolate. Whisk until combined. Whisk in the butter and minced jalapeño.

ASSEMBLY

Place the chocolate dipping sauce in a serving "bowl" set on a serving plate. Arrange a few of each of the mignardises on the plate surrounding the sauce. Serve one plate per table.

The "bowl" that contains the chocolate sauce is actually three interlocking sugar triangles. The triangles are exactly alike, though they don't need to be. To construct the "bowl," place the triangles one atop the other, exactly congruent. Then fan them out. Put the first two at an angle—the more severe the angle the more deep the bowl; you can submerge them in a bowl of granulated sugar to support them while you pour warm liquid sugar down the crease to join them. Add the third, and join it in a similar manner. The triangles meet roughly in the center of one long side.

BLUEBERRY FINANCIER WITH TOASTED LEMON VERBENA SABAYON AND MASCARPONE SHERBET

BO FRIBERG

Chef Instructor, *The Culinary Institute of America at Greystone, St. Helena, California.*

The sweeping, interlocking crescent cookies give this simple, classic dessert a dramatic, attention-getting appeal. A pleasantly tart hint of lemon permeates this dessert, as the custardy financier is accompanied by toasted lemon verbena sabayon and lemon-touched mascarpone sherbet.

YIELD: 16 SERVINGS

Special Equipment:
Sixteen 3" (7.6 cm) diameter x 2" (5 cm) high metal cake rings
One 4 to 4 1/2" (10 to 11.4 cm) diameter tube or bain-marie insert or curved strip of aluminum

BLUEBERRY FINANCIER

1 lb	454 g	unsalted butter
1 pt	473 ml	fresh blueberries, cleaned
18 oz	510 g	confectioners' sugar
5.5 oz	156 g	all-purpose flour
5 oz	142 g	almond meal
14.7 oz	417 g	egg whites
2 Tbs	12 g	finely grated lemon zest
2 oz	57 g	lemon verbena, finely diced

1. Preheat oven to 325°F (165°C). Butter the interior of the ring molds and place on a parchment-lined sheet pan.

2. Place the butter in a skillet and cook over low heat until golden brown (buerre noisette stage), about 5 minutes.

3. Sift together the confectioners' sugar and flour. Blend in the almond meal. Place in a mixer fitted with a paddle attachment. While mixing on low speed, add the egg whites and blend until incorporated. Scrape down the side of the bowl and gradually mix in the buerre noisette. Beat at high speed until well combined. Mix in the lemon zest and verbena.

4. Remove the bowl from the mixer stand and gently fold in the blueberries by hand, being careful not to crush them. Divide the batter equally among the prepared cake rings and bake for about 25 minutes, or until the tops of the cakes feel firm. Allow to cool slightly before removing the cake rings. Invert the baked cakes, cover, and set aside.

Note. Blueberry Financier should be served at room temperature, but may be prepared through step 4 up to two days in advance, if stored in the refrigerator.

LEMON VERBENA SABAYON			
	24 liq oz	*710 ml*	*champagne or dry white wine*
	2 oz	*57 g*	*lemon verbena, finely diced*
	7.8 oz	*221 g*	*egg yolks*
	12 oz	*340 g*	*granulated sugar*

1. In a medium saucepan, combine the champagne or wine with the lemon verbena and heat to about 180°F (82°C); do not boil. Remove from the heat and set aside to infuse for at least 30 minutes, but preferably longer.

2. In a stainless steel mixer bowl, using the whisk attachment, beat the egg yolks and sugar together at high speed until light and fluffy. Strain the wine mixture and then whisk it into the egg yolk mixture.

3. Place the mixer bowl over simmering water and continue to whisk constantly until the sabayon is hot and thick and reaches approximately 160°F (71°C).

> *Note.* If the sabayon must be prepared ahead of time, cook it to 180°F (82°C) to create a more stable mixture. Remove it from the heat and continue to whip until the sauce has cooled to the point where it no longer feels warm to the touch.

CRESCENT DECORATIONS			
	6 oz	*170 g*	*unsalted butter, softened*
	6 oz	*170 g*	*confectioners' sugar, sifted*
	6.3 oz	*179 g*	*egg whites, at room temperature*
	1 tsp	*4 g*	*vanilla extract*
	6 oz	*170 g*	*cake flour, sifted*
	1 tsp	*2 g*	*unsweetend cocoa powder*

1. Preheat oven to 400°F (205°C). In a mixer fitted with a paddle attachment, cream the butter and confectioners' sugar together. Incorporate the egg whites one at a time. Add the vanilla. Add the flour, and mix just until incorporated; do not overmix.

2. Store the paste covered in the refrigerator if not using right away. The paste will keep for several weeks. Allow it to soften slightly after removing it from the refrigerator and then stir it until it is smooth and of a spreadable consistency before using.

3. Cut out a crescent template (see photo on facing page).

4. Place 2 Tbs of the cookie paste in a small container. Add the cocoa powder and stir until completely smooth. Cover and reserve.

5. Place the template on top of a silicone mat. Spread a thin layer of the plain paste over the template and then lift it off. Repeat until you have about 40 cookies (two are used for each serving and some will inevitably break).

6. Place a portion of the reserved cocoa-colored paste into a parchment cone and cut a very small opening. Pipe a curved design on top of the cookies as shown in the drawing.

7. Bake one sheet at a time until halfway done, about 3 minutes. Remove from the oven and cut two holes in the center of each cookie on the top and bottom of the curve using a #2 plain piping tip. Return to the oven and continue baking until the cookie just begins to turn golden brown.

CHOCOLATE MARQUISE WITH PASSION FRUIT PARFAIT AND LACE COOKIE BOUQUET

BO FRIBERG

Chef Instructor, *The Culinary Institute of America at Greystone, St. Helena, California.*

A chocolate marquise, normally prepared in a loaf pan, is given the Modernist, vertical treatment by Chef Friberg. Prepared in PVC-type pipe, this rich chocolate dessert can be (but does not have to be) frozen, so that it can be unmolded easily. As it is unmolded, it is shaped by alternating 45- and 90-degree cuts. It is served with passion fruit parfait and a lace cookie bouquet. "The trick is to make it look showy for the customer, to have them ask, 'How does he do it anyway?'" says Chef Friberg.

YIELD: 12 SERVINGS

Special Equipment:
Two clear plastic pipes that are 22" (55 cm) long and 1 1/2" (3.7 cm) in diameter
Cardboard egg carton
6 to 8" (15 to 20 cm) wide trowel (such as used to apply plaster)

CHOCOLATE MARQUISE	*1 pound, 5 oz*	*595 g*	*sweet dark chocolate*
FILLING	*4.5 oz*	*128 g*	*unsweetened chocolate*
	30 liq oz	*887 ml*	*heavy cream*
	3.9 oz	*111 g*	*egg yolks*
	2 oz	*57 g*	*granulated sugar*
	4 oz	*113 g*	*honey*
	2 liq oz	*59 ml*	*Frangelico liqueur*

1. Chop the sweet and unsweetened chocolates into small chunks. Place in a bowl set over simmering water and melt together. Set aside, but keep warm.

2. Whip the heavy cream to soft peaks; set aside.

3. In mixer fitted with a whisk attachment, beat the egg yolks with the sugar at high speed for about 2 minutes, until light and fluffy. Meanwhile, in a small saucepan, bring the honey to a boil and gradually pour it into the yolks while whipping. Continue to beat the yolks until completely cooled.

4. Fold in the reserved chocolate and the Frangelico. Quickly stir in the whipped cream.

Barry Callebaut
St. Albans Town Industrial Park
RD #2, Box 7
St. Albans, VT 05478-9126
800-556-8845
imported and domestic chocolate couvertures, praline paste, molds and more

Beryl's Cake Decorating Equipment
P.O. Box 1584
N. Springfield, VA 22151
703-256-6951; 800-488-2749
tools for wedding cakes, chocolate work, and confectionery work

Braun Brush Company
43 Albertson Avenue
Albertson, NY 11507
516-741-6000; 800-645-4111
extensive line of brushes for the baking industry; custom-made brushes

Bridge Kitchenware Corp.
214 E. 52nd Street
New York, NY 10022
212-838-6746; 800-274-3435
$3 for catalogue, refundable with first purchase
bakeware, pastry equipment, molds, cake rings

The Candy Factory
12530 Riverside Drive
N. Hollywood, CA 91607
818-766-8220
$5 for catalogue, refundable with first purchase
candy molds, custom molds, flavoring oils, colors

The Chef's Collection
10631 Southwest 146th Place
Miami, FL 33186
800-590-CHEF
brand-name professional cookware, cutlery, gourmet accessories

A Cook's Wares
211 37th Street
Beaver Falls, PA 15010
412-846-9490
chocolate, extracts, bakeware

Creative Culinary Tools
264 SE 46th Terrace
Cape Coral, FL 33904
813-549-7715; 800-340-7278
custom silkscreens, molds, grilles, mold-making compound

DeChoix Specialty Foods
58-25 52nd Avenue
Woodside, NY 11377
718-507-8080; 800-834-6881
chocolate, fruit purées and pastes, nuts and nut products

Demarle, Inc., USA
2666-B Rte 130 N
Cranbury, NJ 08512
609-395-0219
silpats, flexipan, custom flexipans, bread mats and forms

Gourmail
126A Pleasant Valley, #401
Methuen, MA 01844
800-366-5900 ext 96
chocolate

Gourmand
2869 Towerview Road
Herndon, VA 22071
703-708-0000; 800-627-7272
chocolate, flavorings, extracts, pastes

Harry Wils and Co., Inc.
182 Duane Street
New York, NY 10013
212-431-9731
no UPS-delivery within 75 miles of New York City
fruit purées, IQF fruit, chocolate, extracts, nuts and nut products

Holcraft Collection
P.O. Box 792
Davis, CA 95616
916-756-3023
chocolate molds, antique molds

Hygo
P.O. Box 267
Lyndhurst, NJ 07071
201-507-0447; 800-672-9727
disposable pastry bags for cold and hot fillings

Industrial Plastics Supply Co.
309 Canal Street
New York, NY 10013
212-226-2010
plastic demi-spheres, tubing, grilles

INDEX